THE
DESERT

CALIFORNIA STATE SERIES

THE DESERT

Adapted by the Editors of Silver Burdett

from a volume in the LIFE Nature Library

by A. Starker Leopold and the Editors of LIFE

PUBLISHED BY
California State Department of Education
SACRAMENTO, 1967

ON THE COVER: In the early spring, desert bushes burst into bloom in the Borrego Valley in Southern California. The plants with the clublike stems are cholla (choy-yuh) cactuses, which will have flowers in a week or two. There are more color pictures of cactuses in Chapters 3 and 6.

Contents

Preface

Of all the skills that teachers are called upon to develop in their pupils, none rivals reading in importance. Increasingly, without in any way minimizing the role of the basal reading program and its supplements, many educators are calling attention to the far-reaching influence that other books have on reading education. As every teacher knows, pupils cannot become truly competent, well-rounded readers if they are not exposed, under the teacher's guidance, to a variety of reading and reading-related experiences. In many cases this is beyond the scope of the basal program. The Silver Burdett READING AND RESEARCH PROGRAM, developed to help children toward greater reading achievement, provides them with just such experiences.

All the books of this program have characteristics that are unique among reading materials for the elementary grades. They are not textbooks, yet they are books in which content is of such importance that they appeal to the child's overriding interest in his world and thereby enlist him in furthering his own reading education. The READING AND RESEARCH PROGRAM promotes two important, lifelong educational habits. First, through inclusion of material of high interest to the child, the program encourages *independent reading.* Second, through skillful guidance in elementary research experiences, it encourages *reading for learning.*

The books are based upon works by outstanding authorities and have been carefully adapted to preserve the flavor and authenticity of the originals. Topics are treated in depth. They both stimulate and satisfy the inquiring young mind. The child's success in reading is rewarded as his power to comprehend new knowledge grows. His ability to appreciate combinations of words and pictures will equip him for the delights of more adult reading.

In THE DESERT, as in other books of this program, the language is largely familiar to the reader. The enrichment vocabulary that is special to the subject, however, has not been changed, but has been carefully explained so that understanding—a prime requisite for maintaining interest—is assured. All chapters in THE DESERT include both text and picture essays, each calling for a different kind of reading. Paintings and photographs—many of them in color—invite the reader into the book and provide him with a special kind of experience—that of interpreting visual information.

The chief use of each book in the READING AND RESEARCH PROGRAM is within the classroom by groups of pupils. Each book lends itself to oral reading, but its maximum effectiveness lies in other uses. The most important of these is built around research projects appropriate to the grade level and planned in such a way that teacher direction and supervision need not be extensive.

In the Teacher's Guide, the resourceful teacher will find many ways in which the elements of research may be introduced. Specially prepared worksheets are also available for research projects. The worksheets do more than help develop reading comprehension; they underscore the many values that can be derived from intelligent reading of such material. They guide *independent* research activities for individuals and groups. They instruct in research techniques, provide actual research experiences, and open the door to further reading and research.

Through the use of these worksheets, the child will develop a healthy impatience for incomplete information and for readings that preclude full intellectual participation. He will develop the skills of critical reading: drawing inferences, distinguishing between fact and opinion, coping with writing style, recognizing the completeness or incompleteness of evidence, reconstructing the author's argument. The Teacher's Guide contains answers to questions and suggestions for evaluating the pupil's work, but the required teacher participation in pupil research is minimal.

In addition to its research uses, THE DESERT will be welcomed in the classroom for another reason. It can be utilized by pupils and teacher alike as a science source book. The Teacher's Guide provides detailed suggestions for carrying out this purpose.

Recent innovations in the teaching of arithmetic and science have shown that the abilities of children often have been underestimated and that the appeal to pupils of powerful ideas has not been exploited. The READING AND RESEARCH PROGRAM challenges the abilities of all students and provides them with the inspiration and direction to seek further knowledge.   —THE EDITORS

Wind-rippled drifts of white sand
(*left*), like waves on a pond, stretch
across the desert landscape at New
Mexico's White Sands National
Monument. A single yucca plant
casts its shadow on the hot sands.

1

The Driest Places on Earth

The year was 1850, and the United States was not even a hundred years old. Very little was known about the southwestern part of the country. For example, few people knew that much of this region was an area of deserts.

But quite by accident, one woman became an explorer of sorts in this part of the country. Her name was Mrs. Clara Bennett, and she was one of a handful of people who discovered a small but very special place in California.

One morning in 1850, Mrs. Bennett was standing on a high slope in the green Panamint Mountains of eastern California. She had just finished making her journey of discovery. Now she turned to look back toward where she had been.

"Goodbye, Death Valley," she said.

That is how the place was named. Have you ever heard of Death Valley? It is not very large—only about 50 miles long and 20 to 25 miles wide. It is like a huge hole in the ground. In fact, it is the lowest spot in the whole United States—282 feet below sea level. Of course it is a desert—the most terrible sort of desert.

The heat there can be unbearable. The highest temperature ever recorded in the United States was set in Death Valley in 1913—134° in the shade. The bottom of Death Valley is covered with salt, washed down from the mountains all around. Until recent times, in all of Death Valley's 1,000 square miles there were no living things—no plants and no animals.

Pioneers in Death Valley

On that morning in 1850, Mrs. Bennett and her family and several other people had just crossed Death Valley. They were pioneers from the East who had lost their way. They came upon the valley by chance and were the first to make the journey across it. The trip was like a nightmare. Many of the party died of thirst and starvation. Their food and water ran out, and the oxen which pulled their covered wagons died. That is why Mrs. Bennett named the place Death Valley.

Another woman, named Mrs. Rebecca Brier, recorded part of the journey: "Poor little Kirk, my eldest boy, aged nine,

THE DESERTS: THEIR LOCATIONS AND CAUSES

The world's major desert areas and the main forces that cause them are shown on the map at right. In general, these deserts are found in the vicinity of the Tropic of Cancer and the Tropic of Capricorn. Here, the usual or prevailing winds are very dry. In some areas, such as along the coasts of South America and off the coast of North Africa, there are cold ocean currents. The winds which blow inland off these cold currents have very little water in them, and they bring almost no rain to the land. In some areas, there are mountains which cause the winds to lose their moisture near the coast (see text). This is partly the case with North American deserts. Finally, some deserts, like the Gobi, are so far removed from oceans that they get almost no rain.

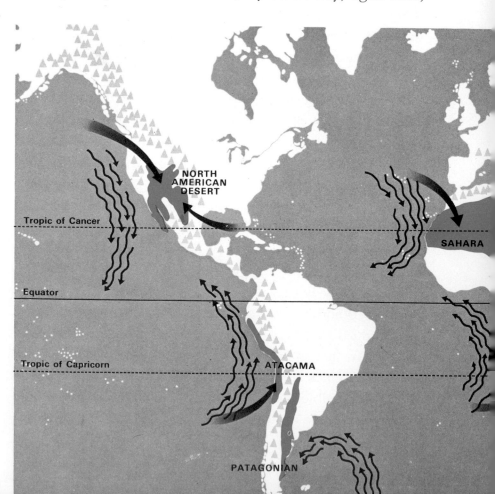

gave out, and I carried him on my back, barely seeing where I was going. [Finally he would say] 'Mother, I can walk now.' Poor little fellow! He would stumble on over the salty marsh for a time and then again sink down crying, 'I cannot go any farther. . . .' Then I would carry him again."

Mrs. Brier's story continues: "Many times I thought I would faint, as my strength would give out, and I would stumble to my knees. The little ones would beg for a drop of water, but we had none to give them."

But a few of these pioneers did make it to safety. They settled down in a fertile valley in California and lived for many years. However, their story of crossing Death Valley is the sort of story we think of when we think about deserts.

A Modern Desert Adventure

But, you may say, that happened long ago. People know about deserts now and know how to get along in them. That is true. But there is still danger.

Only a few years ago, a family set out in their car to go

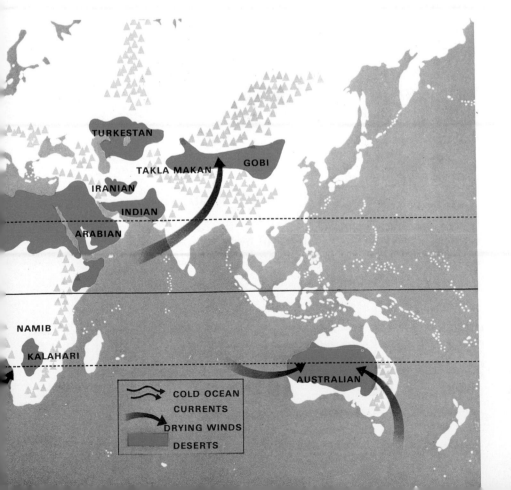

sightseeing in the desert wastelands of southern Utah. They had gone a short distance off the main road when their car broke down.

Now, of course, they had not expected anything to go wrong, and so they had neither food nor water. And even though they were only 50 miles from a town, nobody there knew they were in trouble. And naturally, nobody knew where they were.

These eight people—the father, mother and six children—spent only two days in the desert before they were rescued. But those two days were horrible.

The temperature was so high during the day that the family had to crawl under their car to get some shade. Even there the heat was more than they could stand, so they dug themselves burrows in the ground under the car and lay there during the fierce daytime heat.

They got so hungry during their second day that the mother of the family gave the children some coloring crayons to eat. Later each of them ate about a spoonful of white glue they happened to have in the car.

The Dangers of the Desert

But water, of course, was the biggest problem. Finally they became so thirsty the father drained the rusty water out of the car's radiator and they drank that. And they were glad to have it.

They were sure they were going to die—just when a rescue plane spotted them.

These two cases—the pioneers in Death Valley and the family lost in the desert of Utah—are examples of people who found themselves in trouble in the desert because they were not prepared. They didn't know the dangers of the deserts, or they may have been foolish and ignored them.

RAIN IN DIFFERENT PLACES

The yearly rainfall in five types of climates in the world is shown below. In a tropical rain forest, for example, some 80 inches of rain falls each year. A desert, however, gets only about six inches a year.

TROPICAL RAIN FOREST

JUNGLE

FOREST LANDS

PRAIRIE LANDS

DESERT

But there are many people in the world who have lived their entire lives in deserts. Their fathers and mothers and grandparents and great-grandparents lived in deserts. In fact, there are people living in deserts who actually do not know that much of the world is covered with grass and green trees. To them, the state of Minnesota, which has more than 10,000 lakes, would be impossible to imagine. The reason is that they have become so used to the shortage of water that they cannot imagine a whole lake full of it—much less 10,000 lakes.

How Desert People Feel

More than anybody else, these desert dwellers are aware of the dangers in the desert. They never take any unnecessary chances. In fact, some of them are actually afraid of the desert, even though they live right in the heart of it. For this reason, they may spend their entire lives close to the oasis where they were born. Here there is water and food and shelter from the sun. These are the three most important things in the desert.

We shall learn more about these desert people later. For this is a book about deserts. In the chapters and in the pictures that follow we are going to learn a great many things about deserts.

We shall learn how deserts are created in the first place. We shall see how any area of the world may be turned into a desert because of a change in climate, and why.

We shall take a look at the desert plants and discover how they manage to live in places where there is almost no water. We shall also take a careful look at the different kinds of animals that live in the deserts. We shall learn how very important water is in the desert, and how it can change things in the desert.

Finally, we shall study the people of the desert. These include not only the people who have always lived in deserts, but also people who are now moving from cities and farms to live in the deserts—even Death Valley, the same place the pioneers in 1850 found so terrible.

Here at the beginning of our story we would do well to say

BY DAY, DESERTS SOAK UP MORE HEAT THAN MOIST AREAS

DESERTS IN DAYTIME

The air above deserts is so clear that almost all of the sun's rays are able to reach and heat the ground. Clouds and dust particles in the air prevent only about 10 per cent of these rays from getting through.

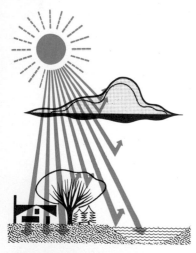

HUMID AREAS IN DAYTIME

In areas of normal rainfall, less than half the sun's rays reach the ground. All the rest are prevented from reaching the ground by dust and clouds in the air—and by the plant life which covers the ground.

exactly what a desert is. Let's begin by trying to imagine.

When somebody mentions an elephant or a table or a lake or a telephone, right away we get a picture in our minds of these things. But suppose somebody says to you, "Imagine a desert." What do you think of? Probably you think of sand and emptiness and cactuses. Maybe you see a line of camels led by some strange men all wrapped up in robes even though it is terribly hot.

If that's what you see when somebody says the word "desert," you are right. Deserts do have sand, and they are empty places with cactuses and camels and men who wear long, flowing robes.

But not all deserts are this way. For example, some deserts have almost no sand at all. Instead, they are covered mostly with rock. And the idea that deserts are always very hot is wrong, too. In some deserts of the world it can get bitterly cold. In fact, some experts consider parts of the Arctic and Antarctic to be deserts. These are so-called "frozen deserts."

The experts are very exact when they define a desert. They say it is a place where the rainfall is less than 10 inches a year. In other words, if the rain did not soak into the ground, it would cover the land to a depth of 10 inches. Deserts are also places of high temperature, where 120° is common. To see the difference between a desert and the sort of place where most people live, we can make a comparison with Baltimore, Maryland. Here the rainfall amounts to about three and a half feet a year, and the average temperature is a rather cool 57°.

The Different Deserts

Probably the best way to realize the differences between the major deserts of the world is to study them one by one.

Of course we will begin with the great Sahara of Africa. The word "Sahara" itself means "desert" in the Arabic language. The Sahara is nearly three times as big as any other desert in the world. It covers 3,500,000 square miles, an area nearly as large as all 50 of the United States.

The Sahara is famous for its huge sand dunes, but the fact is that they cover only one tenth of the Sahara's surface.

There are actually more mountains than sand dunes in the Sahara. Some of these mountains are more than 10,000 feet high. Their peaks are cold and covered with snow. In contrast, the highest temperature ever recorded on earth—136° in the shade—was registered in the Sahara. The rainfall there amounts to only one inch a year.

The driest desert in the world is in South America. It is the Atacama (A-ta-*ka*-ma), which lies partly in Chile and partly in Peru. This long, narrow desert gets less than half an inch of rain a year.

But the strange thing about the Atacama Desert is that it lies directly alongside the Pacific Ocean. For this reason, the climate of the Atacama Desert is very foggy. But it takes more than fog to make plants grow—and the Atacama gets almost no rain to soak into the ground.

The Great Australian Desert

The second biggest desert in the world is the desert of Australia. It covers 1,300,000 square miles, which is nearly half the size of the Australian continent. Compared with the Atacama or the Sahara, the Australian is a "wet" desert, since it gets about five inches of rain a year.

This desert is so large that huge parts of it have never been explored. In fact, it wasn't until 1955 that some travelers happened upon a group of people there that nobody had known about before. They were the Bindibu tribesmen, who have made their home in the Australian desert for thousands of years.

The great deserts of North America, which include those in the United States, rank fifth in size among the deserts of the world. They cover 500,000 square miles. Perhaps the most outstanding thing about these deserts is their rock formations. These include great natural bridges hundreds of feet long, carved in the rock by ages of erosion.

One of the most famous deserts in the world is the Gobi (*Go*-bee), which is partly in Mongolia and partly in China. It was one of the first deserts to be crossed by explorers from the outside world. Marco Polo, the well-known traveler from Venice, Italy, made his way across the Gobi during the 1300s.

DESERTS TURN COLD AT NIGHT, AND WETTER LANDS REMAIN WARM

DESERTS AT NIGHT

At night, the desert floor loses the huge amount of heat it received during the day. Only about 10 per cent is prevented from escaping by layers of dust particles in the air above the now cool desert floor.

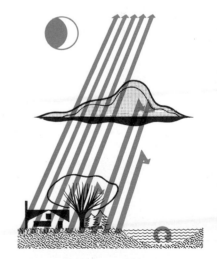

HUMID AREAS AT NIGHT

At night in areas with normal rain, the ground loses only about half of the heat received during the day. The rest is prevented from escaping by the dust and clouds in the air —and by the plants on the ground.

15

Even that long ago, the Gobi was famous as a place of danger for travelers.

Marco Polo was warned not to take more than 50 people in his caravan, because there were not enough sources of water in the Gobi to supply a larger party.

But the Gobi was not always a place without water. Scientists have discovered the remains of prehistoric dinosaur eggs there. These dinosaurs ate plants, which suggests that the Gobi was once a rainy place with much plant life.

But while some deserts like the Gobi and the Sahara were drying up, at least one area was becoming partly covered by water. This was the vast Turkestan Desert in the southern part of the Soviet Union. "Turkestan" means "land of the Turks." A portion of this desert borders the Caspian Sea.

The Caspian Sea is actually a salty inland lake—the largest in the world. It nearly dried up about 6,000 years ago for lack of water. However, about 4,000 years ago, there was a change of climate in the area and the Caspian Sea filled up again. When it did, its waters spread over at least one community that had been built on the shores of the lake when it was much smaller. Today it is possible to look down into 10 feet of water and see the remains of the houses built thousands of years ago.

But the Turkestan Desert is still very dry. It covers 750,000 square miles and is the fourth largest desert in the world. The Arabian Desert (1,000,000 square miles) is third largest.

The Importance of Deserts

These, then, are most of the important deserts of the world. All together, deserts cover one seventh of the land surface of the earth. In other words, if all the deserts in the world were grouped into one spot, they would cover an area larger than the continent of South America.

Since the world's deserts take up so much land, and since the population of the world is growing, these desert areas are becoming more and more important. It would be a wonderful thing if the deserts could be put to use. And slowly we are learning how this may be done.

Now let us see how deserts are formed in the first place.

CHILDREN OF THE TEDA TRIBE, IN THE SOUTH SAHARA, PLAY NEAR THEIR VILLAGE OF MAT-COVERED HUTS

A Look at the Sahara

The Sahara, world's greatest desert, covers three and a half million square miles, nearly a third of the African continent. It is mostly bare rock and dry dunes, but it also has mountains 10,000 feet high and a lake as big as the state of New Jersey. It is the home of more than three million people.

17

A MOUNTAINOUS DUNE rises high above the desert floor in the wasteland of the southeastern Sahara. Dunes like this one may be many miles long and often more than 500 feet high. Three things are needed to form a dune: there must be plenty of sand, a steady wind and an obstacle—a rock or plant—around which sand may slowly

collect. When the wind blows steadily against such an obstacle, a long-sloped crescent of sand builds up on the side toward the wind. On the other side, the dune drops off as a sharp, curving cliff. Dunes, though frequently thought of as symbols of deserts, are actually not too common and cover only a small portion of the Sahara.

A DESERT CITY, Beni Isguen covers a hill in the parched Mzab Valley of the Sahara in northern Africa. Built in the 11th Century, the city shows people can prosper in the desert. Beni Isguen gets its water from thousands of wells dug down 120 feet deep through solid limestone. These wells are used to irrigate large palm tree groves.

A HERD OF CAMELS gathers by a shallow but famous water hole in Chad, an inland country of north-central Africa. At times of great drought, when all other nearby sources of water are dry, this oasis in the Archai Canyon never fails to provide a trickle of water. The canyon is so remote that it was not discovered until the early 1920s.

21

ISLANDS OF ROCK rise from the floor of the Sahara near the southern border of Libya, a country in north Africa. The odd rocky formations are all that remain of an ancient plateau formed many millions of years ago when this area was covered by ocean waters. Mud and sand from the surrounding uplands were washed down and

settled on the ocean floor. In time, the large plateau thus formed built up to a height of 1,000 feet. Then, about 350 million years ago, shifts in the surface of the earth lifted up this entire area so that it was above water —and the erosion process began. It has gone on ever since, leaving only these lonely rocky clumps and spires.

23

AN ANCIENT FORT, deep within the Sahara, stands close by its vital oasis at El Goléa, Algeria. The fort was constructed by Arabs 1,100 years ago, when raiders were roaming the desert. It is now abandoned except for huge numbers of roosting bats.

24

A natural arch soars over Indian
herders and sheep in Monument
Valley of Arizona. The opening was
made by water which froze in the
stone, then expanded, gradually
flaking off pieces of the surface.

2

How Deserts
Are Created

Something almost frightening comes to mind when you
think of the Sahara. It is as if the name itself could make a
person thirsty. Here is this enormous area—nearly as big as
the entire United States—and it is an almost lifeless wasteland of rock and sand and heat. In all its 3.5 million square
miles, there are only a few plants and trees, and only a handful of determined people are able to live there.

Yet it was not always so. At one time—long ago—vast
stretches of the Sahara were green forests.

Then, over the ages, there was a change in the climate of
the region, and slowly the Sahara became drier and drier.

Under certain conditions, any region of the earth could
become a desert. A lack of rain for a very long time is all
that is really needed. Therefore, it is climate which is the
deciding factor in the creation of a desert.

Here it should be remembered that there is a difference
between *weather* and *climate*. Weather occurs day by day.
There are rainy days and sunny days. But climate is the
weather pattern over a long period. It is the year-in, year-out
type of weather characteristic of a region.

EROSION IN DESERTS

The earth's surface, which seems so unmoving and unmovable, in fact is changing constantly but very slowly. Over millions of years, some areas sink. But others may be lifted up and thereby exposed to erosion.

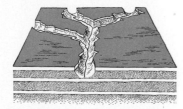

Under desert conditions, a newly uplifted plain is marked by a few steep-sided valleys, usually cut by swift-flowing streams. The Grand Canyon in Arizona is an excellent example of this stage of erosion.

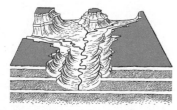

Many thousands of years later, the same area will look quite different. The process of erosion will have carved deep, broad valleys, leaving buttes and mesas standing alone. This kind of terrain occurs in Utah.

The final stage in desert erosion comes when the land has been so worn down that few distinct features remain. Such drab areas have occurred in the past, but there are none on earth at the present time.

What is it, then, that accounts for a dry desert climate? There are several things. Probably the easiest to understand is the "rain shadow."

To have a rain shadow, there must first be a range of coastal mountains. In addition, there must also be a steady, prevailing warm wind blowing inland over the mountains. The land which lies beyond the mountains is said to be in a rain shadow. The process works like this:

The winds sweeping inland off the ocean are full of moisture. They strike the mountains and are forced upward. As the air rises, it also cools. Cool air cannot hold as much moisture as warm air. So this cooled air drops its moisture as rain. In this way, the seacoast side of the mountains receives large amounts of rain.

By the time the wind has finally crossed the mountains, it has lost almost all the moisture it once held. There is none left for the land beyond, which is said to be in the rain shadow of the mountains.

This is exactly what happens in the far western United States. Moist winds blowing off the Pacific Ocean must cross the mountains of the Coast Ranges and then the giant Sierra Nevada. During their journey across these mountains, the winds lose almost all their moisture. Thus the seaward side of the mountains receives a great deal of rain, and some of the mightiest forests in this country are found there. But there is no moisture left for the inland regions.

The result is a vast dry area which covers all of Nevada and parts of California.

Isolated Deserts

The second situation which can produce desert conditions is something like a rain shadow—only without the mountains. This can happen when a region is located a great distance from an ocean. The huge Gobi Desert of Mongolia is such a region. It lies far inland and the winds which sweep across it are very dry. They have traveled overland so long they have lost all the moisture they once had.

Even a region lying directly alongside the ocean may be turned into a desert. This occurs in coastal areas when the waters offshore are part of a cold ocean current. The winds which blow across these cold stretches of water become cooled themselves, and cannot hold very much moisture.

The cold winds blowing inland usually carry only enough water to produce fog—but no rain. An example of such a region is the coast of Peru, which borders the Pacific Ocean. It is a very foggy region. But it is also extremely dry, because little rain—and in some years, none—ever falls there.

The Air Currents

Among the various forces which can turn an area into a desert, by far the most important influences are the patterns followed by vast air currents moving around the earth.

To understand how this works, you must first realize that there are zones of climate in different parts of the world. Much of the United States, for example, is in a zone where there are frequent changes. In such a place, the weather is often hard to predict. In other places, however, the climate is such that the weather changes very little from day to day and even month to month. Malaya is one such place. It has a decidedly wet climate all year long.

Such different zones of climate are the result of these great masses of air which circulate about the earth. From one season to another, these huge atmospheric rivers of air shift somewhat. However, their general flow usually follows well-established patterns.

Thus, Malaya gets a tremendous amount of rain because it happens to be located in an area where moist, warm air is rising and cooling. As a result, the water in the rising air condenses and falls as rain. Malaya is therefore located in a zone of almost constant wet weather.

But vast regions of the earth unfortunately happen to lie in areas beyond these zones of wet weather. Here, the air high overhead is cool and has shed its moisture in a wet-weather zone. Because it is cool, the air is heavy, and flows back down toward earth.

As the air descends, it begins to warm up—and the lower it gets, the hotter it gets. What happens to the land below is a kind of double tragedy: naturally, the dry descending

EROSION IN MOIST REGIONS

In areas of normal rainfall, land is also subject to erosion after it has been uplifted by movements in the earth's surface. But here, erosion produces a different type of scenery than is found in deserts.

In moist regions, rains are frequent but moderate, and there is plant life to hold the topsoil. Erosion makes V-shaped valleys whose sides are gently sloping. An example is New York's Hudson River Valley.

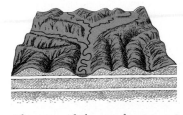

After several thousand years, original valleys have broadened and new streams have cut the land so that it is quite hilly. This type of landscape is to be found in the Mississippi and Connecticut Valleys.

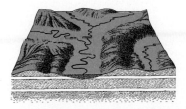

As the erosion process continues, the countryside begins to look like a plain. There are few hills and they are widely spaced. The looping rivers follow twisting courses as the waters flow toward the sea.

29

air fails to bring any rain to the land below. But even worse, because it is so hot and dry, the air actually soaks up whatever little moisture there may be on the ground. In this way, the already parched earth is wrung even drier.

The Fate of the Sahara

So far we have talked about four kinds of desert conditions: (1) An area in the "rain shadow" of some mountains. (2) An area so remote from the ocean that it gets no rain. (3) A coastal area lying alongside a cold ocean current where onshore winds pick up only enough moisture to form fog. (4) And most important, a region swept by dry air coming down from a great altitude.

Any one of these four factors is enough to produce desert conditions. But some areas are afflicted by two or more. The forbidding Sahara is certainly a good illustration.

First of all, the Sahara lies in an area of dry, moistureless winds. In addition, much of its area is far removed from water. Finally, the cool ocean waters of the Canary Current flow past the northwestern coastal regions of the Sahara. The onshore winds therefore carry little moisture with them.

We said at the beginning of this chapter that deserts themselves are not necessarily permanent and any region can come under the influence of desert conditions. And this is true—though such changes would take place very slowly.

For example, it is possible that the routes of ocean currents could change, and a cold, fog-producing current might be replaced by a warmer one. Mountains which cast a rain shadow can be eroded away. Wind patterns may be altered. Changes of this nature could drench the Sahara with rain, while Malaya might become dry as dust.

Compared with vast ocean currents and huge mountains, the role of man in the creation of deserts may not seem like much. But he often plays an important part.

Many dry regions of the world are kept from becoming real deserts by a light covering of sparse vegetation. These plants protect the soil from the harsh effects of wind and sun. Their roots also help to hold the soil and prevent it from being washed or blown away.

All too often, however, man has disturbed this delicate balance which keeps a poor area from turning into an actual desert. He has foolishly allowed his herds of animals to overgraze and kill off the protective plants. He has also plowed up this natural covering in order to plant crops. Many areas east of the Mediterranean Sea were once livable but have been turned into real deserts in this fashion. And the same thing happened during the 1930s when parts of the southwestern United States were improperly farmed. Millions of tons of topsoil were carried hundreds of miles away by the wind, and the area was turned into what was called the "Dust Bowl."

This part which man plays in helping to convert poor areas into desert regions is well illustrated in the case of the Bedouin tribesmen of Arabia. Suppose a Bedouin woman decided to make a pot of coffee for her husband. In order to collect enough brush for a fire to boil the water, she would have to gather every shrub in an area 100 feet wide by 100 feet long.

Furthermore, if this same Bedouin couple had even a small flock of four sheep, these animals could nibble clean two entire acres of land a day.

How Deserts Age

So far we have dealt with the forces which create deserts. Let us move on now to look at what happens after a region has become a desert.

Scientists say that deserts go through three distinct steps of aging as the land is worn down by erosion: There are young deserts, middle-aged deserts and old deserts.

There is a strange thing about this aging process. As we have learned, the absence of water created the desert in the first place. But once a desert has been formed, water is the chief force in wearing it away.

In this connection, it seems that almost nothing in the deserts ever occurs in moderation. Month after month— even year after year—the pitiless sun glares down on the desert from a cloudless sky.

But storms do come to the deserts, and when they come,

they are usually sudden and furious. Flash floods hurtle down the barren gullies, and the floodwater carries with it vast quantities of sand, loose stones and sometimes even boulders. In a very real sense, these are the "tools" of erosion. They cut and batter at the land, shaping it into wonderfully varied desert land forms.

Many of these strange land forms are due to the fact that all parts of a desert do not wear away at the same rate. Harder material erodes more slowly than softer material. In some deserts, particularly in the southwestern United States, there are large, flat-topped hills rearing above the desert floor. These hills were left standing while the area around them was worn away. Their flat tops are made of very hard stone which protected them. They are called *mesas*, which is a Spanish word meaning "tables."

But in time, even a mesa will wear away and become a smaller, steep-sided hill known as a butte. And buttes themselves in time may erode, leaving nothing more than some tall, chimneylike columns of rock to mark the location of what once may have been a huge plateau.

There would seem to be almost no limit to the wildly differing land forms which this sort of water-produced erosion can create. Probably the best examples of this type of erosion are to be found in the deserts of the southwestern United States, particularly in Utah.

Wind Erosion

But water is not the only erosive force which wears deserts away. Wind, too, does its part—though it is not nearly so effective as water. Like water, wind also uses a "tool" for erosion. This tool is sand.

But sand is comparatively heavy, and even a strong wind can rarely lift it more than a few feet off the ground. The result is that rocks eroded by wind-driven sand are often top-heavy, because the sand has eaten away at their bases. In this same way, unprotected telephone poles are simply cut off at the bottom. Even metal plates are unable to protect these poles for more than a few years.

The times of greatest wind erosion, of course, are during

TRANSVERSE DUNES

Moderate one-way winds (arrows) create dunes which look like waves on a frozen sand sea. And much like slow-moving ocean waves, they creep across the desert. Such dunes occur in places with abundant sand.

LONGITUDINAL DUNES

Stronger one-way winds (arrow) blow the sand into ridges, usually only a few feet high but very often many miles long. Unlike transverse dunes, longitudinal dunes stretch out in the direction of the wind.

the tremendous sandstorms for which the deserts are so famous. There is a popular notion that people trapped in such storms are choked to death by a smothering cloud of sand whipped up by the wind.

Yet the truth is that in real desert sandstorms, most of the sand is lifted at most a few feet above the ground. The sand therefore is like a waist-high cloud, gliding over the desert like a great moving carpet. An adult standing upright finds that he is able to breathe quite freely.

Furthermore, scientists have made studies of the way sand behaves during these storms. It is not blown horizontally across the ground, but each individual grain bounds along with a kind of skipping motion. The wind picks up a grain and hurtles it forward for a distance of perhaps 10 feet. It then strikes the earth and rebounds into the air for another flight of several feet.

Choking Dust Storms

Much more terrifying than sandstorms are the desert dust storms. Since dust is so much lighter than sand, the wind can raise huge clouds of it—clouds so dense that in the center of the storm it is as dark as night.

In a large dust storm, 300 to 400 miles across, the wind may be carrying more than 100 million tons of dust. This would be enough to make a huge hill two miles in diameter at its base and 100 feet high.

The dust in a really big dust storm may be carried by the wind for almost unbelievable distances. For example, reddish dust whipped into the air by winds over the Sahara has been known to settle back to the earth in England. In November 1933, there was a severe dust storm in the Central Plains of the United States, which includes Oklahoma and Kansas. Dust from this huge storm actually discolored the snow in New England, where a fall of 25 tons of dust on each square mile was measured.

These, then, are the main forces which shape the deserts. Fierce but infrequent rains wash down rocks which chip and scour away at other rocks. The force of the winds may move acres and acres of sand, piling it into dunes

BARCHAN DUNES

Steady one-way winds blowing across an area where sand is scarce can build up dunes in the shape of crescent moons. The sand blows more easily over the low tips than over higher areas near the center.

STAR DUNES

In areas where the wind blows from many directions, sand piles up into large, ridged hills. Such dunes can remain in the same place for many centuries and by so doing serve as reliable landmarks for travelers.

which sometimes rise to a height of 700 feet. But in certain desert areas, the winds may eventually sweep the surface free of sand. When this occurs, the ground left behind sometimes looks like a pebbled pavement, polished smooth over the centuries by wind-blown sand.

The "Singing" Sands

One desert mystery which sometimes happens during or after a sandstorm is called the "song" of the sands, though actually it is a strange booming noise.

This booming sound starts when a huge quantity of sand suddenly begins to slide down the side of a dune. The vibrations caused by this avalanche of sand often set off other slides on other dunes.

As the sand tumbles down, the weird booming, or song, is produced. The sound is sometimes like distant thunder, though legend says it is the tolling of bells in a chapel buried under the sand. It may last for five minutes or more, and it sometimes is so loud that people standing alongside one another have to shout to make themselves heard.

One famous student of deserts tells of a slow measurable beat to this strange and rare "music" of the desert. This same scientist tried for a long time to find an explanation for the "singing sands," but never succeeded.

And so we have the deserts. They are forbidding places, certainly. But for many people, they also possess a strange sort of fascination. If nothing else, there is something wonderful about the simple emptiness to be found there. And nowhere on earth are the skies clearer or the nights more filled with stars than on a desert.

There are also the weird but wonderful shapes of rocks. And the colors found in the deserts, and the marvelous patterns of light and shadow are unequaled anywhere.

A French author familiar with the Sahara found that the people who live in deserts come to love their homes more than people in any other place.

"Men will die for a leafless, stony mountain," he wrote. "The nomads will defend to the death their great store of sand as if it were a treasure of gold dust."

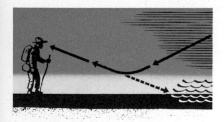

A MIRAGE

This startling desert trick usually makes travelers think they see a pool of water ahead. It works like this: Temperatures on the desert floor may reach 180 degrees. Thus the air above the floor gets very hot. This hot air acts like a wavy-surfaced mirror in which reflections can be seen. The "pond" of water seen in the distance is really only a reflection of the blue sky overhead.

BUTTES—STUMPS OF ROCK REMAINING FROM AN ERODED PLATEAU—STAND IN MONUMENT VALLEY, UTAH

Water and Wind at Work

Deserts are burning hot by day and chilling cold at night. Deserts also have few plants to cover and hold the soil. Thus wind and water have nothing to prevent them from eroding the land. The result is a landscape carved into strange shapes—and some of the most spectacular scenery anywhere.

35

The Geography of a Desert

This is a painting of an imaginary desert landscape, showing many things typical of deserts everywhere. The range of high mountains (*below*) is responsible for the creation of the desert in the first place. Winds off the ocean (*arrow, left*) reach the

FRESH-WATER PIPELINE

SALT REMOVAL PLANT

SNOW FIELD

OCEAN

SNOW-FED STREAMS

WIND

RAIN ON OCEAN SIDE OF MOUNTAINS

INLAND SLOPE IN "RAIN SHADOW"

MOUNTAIN LAKE

PUMPING PLANT   WATER TUNNEL

IRRIGATION PIPELINE

WATER-BEARING LAYER

WATER-BEARING LAYER

MEL HUNTER

mountains and rise. This cools the water-laden clouds which drop their moisture, leaving almost no rain for the inland regions. The result is a desert.

Here we see snow-fed streams cutting gullies and canyons. Lonely buttes and mesas are the eroded stumps of vast plateaus. The salt lake and salt flats are the remains of an ancient inland sea.

Yet man can make the desert bloom by irrigating the land with water obtained from lakes, streams and underground sources.

BUTTE

MESA

SALT FLATS (PLAYA)

SALT LAKE

IRRIGATED FARMLAND

DAM

CANYON

STEEP CLIFF

IRRIGATED LAND

GRAVITY-FED IRRIGATION SYSTEM

NATURAL OASIS

NATURAL WELL

ARTESIAN WELL

Water—the Main Force in Shaping the Desert

Though deserts are known for their dryness, oddly enough they most often are shaped by water working in different ways. For example, water trapped in a rock can split it by freezing and expanding. And

THE COLORADO RIVER, TWISTING ITS WAY THROUGH SOUTHERN UTAH, ALMOST DOUBLES BACK UPON ITSELF.

some kinds of rocks are dissolved by water. But most often, water shapes deserts by using loose stones and gravel washed down by violent rains. These pieces of rock are carried along by swift-flowing waters like the Colorado River (*below*). Rushing downstream, they batter and gouge the land, wearing away layer after layer of rock. The Colorado River has dug its bed 1,300 feet deeper than it was one million years ago.

ITS GENTLY LOOPING COURSE WAS ESTABLISHED LONG AGO. SINCE THEN ITS RATE OF FLOW HAS INCREASED

PINK TOWERS IN UTAH'S BRYCE CANYON ARE ALL THAT REMAIN OF AN ANCIENT LIMESTONE PLATEAU. THEY

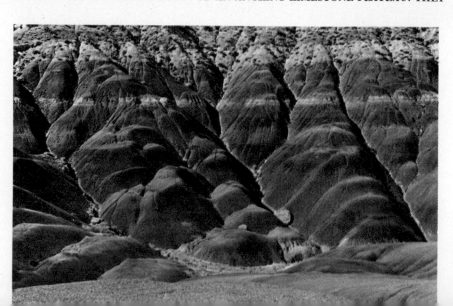

HARD ROCK, like these purple hillocks in New Mexico, resists erosion. Centuries of weathering have left these with only shallow gullies and gently rounded sides.

40

WERE FORMED BY RIVERS WHICH ERODED THE SOFTER ROCK AND LEFT THE MORE DURABLE SPIRES BEHIND

SOFT ROCK and clay of this weathered cliff face in the Borrego Badlands of California are easily cut by erosion. Occasional violent rains have left deep scars in the hillside.

41

A DRIED-UP LAKE BOTTOM, the Bonneville Salt Flats in Utah are certainly one of the flattest places on earth. For thousands of years, dissolved salt from the mountains around has been washed down by spring rains. The water evaporates, leaving the salt behind. These flats are so hard that automobile speed records have been set here.

WHITE DUNES of gypsum, the raw material from ➤ which plaster is made, cover the bottom of New Mexico's Tularosa Basin *(right)*. Like the salt in the picture above, the gypsum crystals are formed by evaporation. Blown by steady winds, the grains of gypsum form dunes sometimes 100 feet high. The area covers 275 square miles.

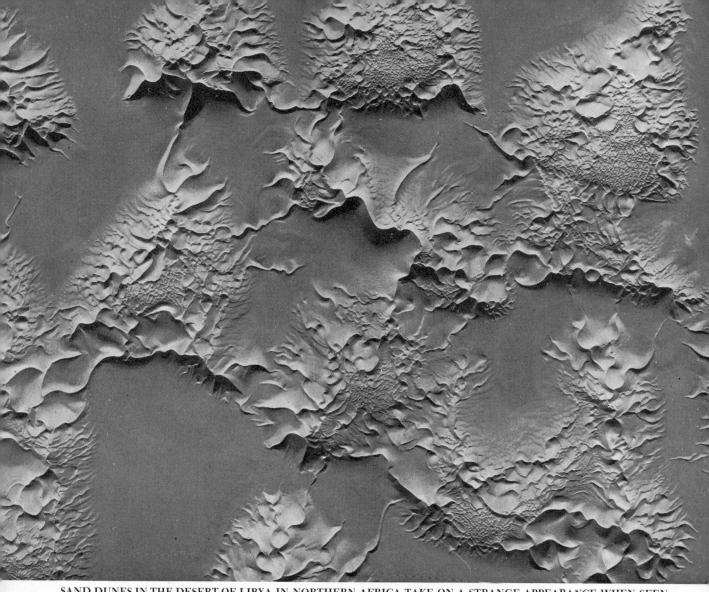

SAND DUNES IN THE DESERT OF LIBYA IN NORTHERN AFRICA TAKE ON A STRANGE APPEARANCE WHEN SEEN

A CLUSTER OF PALMS stands in a hollow around an Algerian oasis. Walls circling the grove are to keep out sand. The picture was taken from an altitude of 600 feet.

AN ARIZONA BUTTE shows the results of erosion on its layers of rock. Clearly visible are the drainage gullies arranged around the center like the spokes of a wheel.

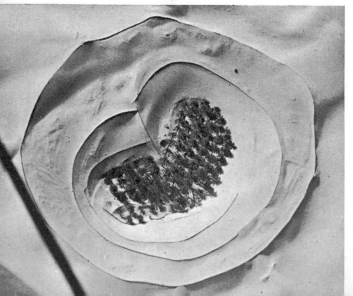

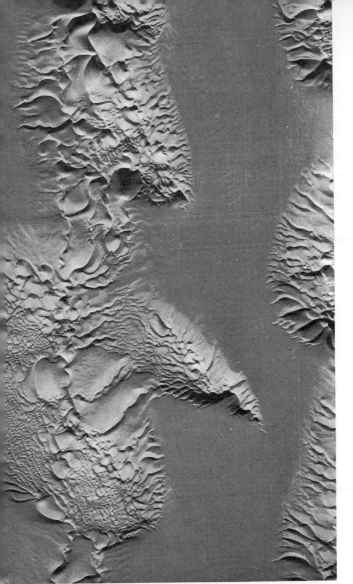

FROM AN AIRPLANE AT AN ALTITUDE OF 32,000 FEET

Desert Patterns Seen from the Air

The wonderfully distinctive shapes of the desert landscape are beautiful from the ground. But when seen from the air, these shapes look entirely different—and often more exciting. Some examples of these amazing desert patterns are shown on these pages. The sand dunes shown at the left look very much like a close-up photograph of some blisters on an old painted wall. In reality they are enormous wind-blown hills of sand in which a person might easily lose his way.

What might be two lacy leaves (*second from the right, below*) is really a dried-up borax deposit seen from a great height. What seems like a bowl with berries in it (*far left, below*) is actually a cluster of palm trees at an Algerian desert oasis. The appearance of a bowl comes from walls built of palm branches and mud to keep the drifting desert sands from clogging this precious oasis. Finally, the cracks in a mud flat (*below*) look like the map of a city.

A BORAX DEPOSIT on the barren floor of Death Valley in California could be a pair of feathery plumes when seen from an airplane flying high above the ground.

A WEB OF CRACKS crisscrosses a drying mud flat in the Colorado Desert. Such cracks appear within only a few hours after heavy rains have drenched the desert floor.

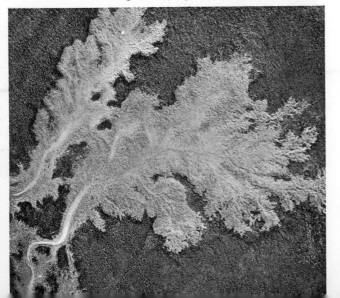

A SLAB OF ROCK is the hardened remains of volcanic lava which seeped up into a crack in the earth. The slab was exposed when the surrounding rock was worn away.

A GIANT STONE PILLAR pokes up out of Utah's Fiery Furnace, named for the redness of the rock. Water eroded the softer sandstone which once surrounded the pillar.

NATURAL ARCH is a dramatic sandstone span 291 feet long and 118 feet above the desert floor near Moab, Utah. It was formed by winter rains seeping into the rock, then

A SCULPTURED ROCK in the Sahara owes its shape to wind-blown sand. Its hourglass shape shows that sand can be lifted only a few feet above the floor of the desert.

freezing and expanding so that pieces of rock flaked off. In time, a hole was worn and slowly enlarged by wind and water erosion and by the sandstone itself falling away.

A SHELTERING CAP of rock tops this column in New Mexico. Over the ages, rain has washed away most of the neighboring stone—except stone underneath the rock.

47

The Nature of Sand

What is sand? Scientists are very exact about the answer. To begin with, sand must be made of rock—most often tiny chips of quartz. Its grains also must be a certain size—no bigger than the head of a pin and not so small as dust. The grains may be rough at first, but then as they are pushed around by wind and water, they get rounder and rounder. Sand grains in the deserts finally look like tiny marbles.

◄ **TRICKLES OF SAND** spill down ledges *(left)* where the Colorado River enters Lake Mead on the Arizona-Nevada border. Because of its weight, the sand carried by rivers moves downstream very slowly, traveling only about half a foot each year. But little river sand ever reaches the sea.

A PYRAMID OF SAND towers above an oasis in the northern Sahara. The desert sand is shifting constantly, so its moving grains always are grinding against each other. After centuries of such movement, a sand grain has been polished to a finish which is like dull ground glass.

High-flying, Choking Dust

A wind strong enough to lift sand grains a few feet off the ground can carry the finer particles of dust high across continents. The dust storms of the southwestern U.S. in the 1930s were the result of very poor farming and grazing practices which killed off the soil-holding plants. There followed a long period of drought and high winds which blew the powdery soil away—850 million tons of it during a single year.

WIND-BLOWN DUST fills the air around members of an Oklahoma family whose farm has been ruined. Many such families had to abandon their homes in the 1930s.

AN ORANGE CLOUD of dust *(right)* moves toward a ➤ farm in northern Texas. Dust can be carried miles high on rising air currents and may be held aloft for weeks.

3

Plants That Live in the Desert

To see one of nature's big surprises, visit one of our American deserts early in the year. After the brief spring rains, the land hardly looks like a desert at all. The ground is carpeted with brilliant flowers—gold, red, purple and orange. The bushes are in bloom, too—and even the cactuses. Everywhere the leaves are green.

But stay in the desert for only a few short weeks and you will see the flowers begin to wither and drop to the ground. Slowly the stems of the plants shrivel. Their leaves fall or turn dry as paper. Even the cactuses begin to shrivel. And once again the desert becomes a wasteland.

The withering away of desert plants may seem strange. But it is really no different from what happens when autumn comes to many other regions. In these areas most growth stops—or at least slows down greatly—as the plants prepare to live through the long, cold winter ahead.

But instead of a cold, snowy winter, desert plants must wait out long periods with no moisture at all—periods which may go on for six months, a year or even many years. In the desert, therefore, we find only those plants which have

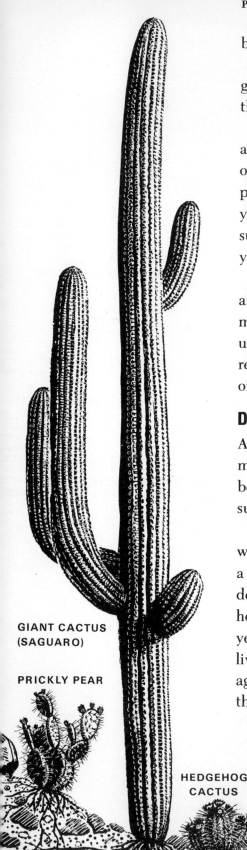

GIANT CACTUS (SAGUARO)

PRICKLY PEAR

HEDGEHOG CACTUS

BARREL CACTUS

OCOTILLO

WINDMILLS

become able to survive under these conditions of climate.

Every plant growing in the desert belongs to one of two groups, depending on the methods it has adopted to endure the desert climate.

The plants of the first group, the "drought survivors," are so named because they stay alive through long periods of dry weather. They are like our familiar trees or garden perennials. Perennials are plants which live from year to year, growing larger every season. In the desert these plants survive from one rainy season to another, growing slowly year by year.

Plants of the second group, called "drought avoiders," are like garden annuals, such as tomatoes and zinnias, which must be planted anew from seeds every year. They spring up after a rain, bloom quickly and die. Only their seeds remain, ready to bring forth new plants after the next period of plentiful rainfall.

Drought Survivors

Among the many types of drought survivors, probably the most interesting are the juicy "succulents," so called because they are full of moisture. The most famous of the succulents by far are the cactuses.

During a walk through one of our American deserts, you would see cactuses of many sizes. Some are no bigger than a thimble. But the giant saguaro—the skyscraper of the desert—may stand as high as 50 feet. To reach such a height, however, takes the saguaro a very long time. A saguaro 50 years old has grown only three feet high. But saguaros also live to be very old—sometimes 200 years or more. At that age they may weigh as much as 10 tons—though most of that weight will be in the form of water.

This large supply of water is gathered by the cactuses

through their roots, which are specially adapted for the purpose. These roots are very long and stretch out over a wide area, just beneath the surface of the ground. So arranged, they are ready to soak up every possible drop of water that falls when the rare desert rains finally come.

But there is little telling when these rains will occur. If the cactuses are to survive, they must be able to store water to keep them alive from one rainy season to the next.

The night-blooming cereus, for example, makes use of a large water-storage container underground. After a season of plentiful rain, some of these underground bulbs will have swollen to such an extent that they weigh 40 pounds.

Most cactuses, however, keep their stored water in their stems. In fact, the characteristic shape of most cactuses you see is simply the result of these plants being almost all stem —except for their thorns. Some varieties have stems made up of many thick pads. The prickly pear is an example. But stems of most cactuses are round—like barrels or spheres.

Like their roots, the shapes of cactuses also serve a specialized desert purpose: since most cactuses are round, they can expand quickly, swelling up as the roots drink in water when it rains. Then later, during the long periods of drought, the cactus stems slowly shrink as the plant draws upon its supply of stored water.

One Problem, Many Solutions

Among the drought survivors, there are several varieties which have leaves. But these particular plants must guard against losing too much moisture through these leaves by evaporation. They do this in a variety of ways.

The leaves of some desert plants are covered with leathery or waxy coatings which slow down evaporation. The leaves of others have fine hairs which serve the same purpose.

MESQUITE

PRIMROSE

NIGHT-BLOOMING CEREUS

THREADPLANT

On other plants only small leaf surfaces are exposed to the sun, since smaller leaves lose less water. The leaves of a paloverde plant, for example, are so tiny that 25 of them laid side by side would cover only one inch of space.

Going a step further, some desert plants save water by shedding their leaves altogether. The thin, whiplike stems of the ocotillo may grow six crops of leaves a year, each crop developing after a period of rain. But at the first sign of drought the leaves are shed quickly.

While the leaves of most plants everywhere produce the food the plant needs, cactuses have no leaves at all. Their food is produced in their green stems. The paloverde—whose Spanish name means "green trunk"—has food-producing leaves. But its stems and twigs can also produce food. In this way the paloverde can go on providing nourishment even when it sheds its leaves because of a long dry spell.

Another device for survival which many desert plants have developed is thorns, which serve at least two purposes. They serve as a means of protecting the plants from being eaten by animals. And they also are useful in providing a small amount of shade from the sun's rays.

Storing Water Underground

Some of the hardiest drought survivors—perhaps as many as one third of this group of plants—endure periods of dryness by what appears to be complete surrender. In times of drought the entire plant above ground simply shrivels and dies. But underground it is very much alive. It lives on the store of food and water contained in underground roots, bulbs or tubers.

Some of these buried storehouses reach an astonishing size. In southern Africa, there is a great desert known as the Kalahari. A spindly vine that grows there springs from a huge underground tuber that may be as big as a basketball. When the Bushmen, a wandering people of the Kalahari, see one of these vines, they carefully note its location. Later, if water cannot be found anywhere else, they return to the spot and dig up the water-filled tuber.

The endless struggle for water by the desert plants has one

curious result that is best seen from the air. Fly over a desert and it almost seems that the trees and shrubs below have been laid out as in a formal garden. That is because they are situated at exact intervals from one another.

The explanation for this gardenlike effect is simple. Each plant has spread its roots in a wide circle, seeking every drop of moisture to be found in the soil around it. No moisture is left inside that circle for other plants to use. Therefore the seeds of other plants that fall inside the circle usually fail to develop. Each shrub or tree thus stands alone, at almost the same distance from each of its neighbors.

Some plants do more than merely soak up all moisture in their area. They actually spread poison to keep other plants from growing too close to them. Two American desert shrubs, the brittlebush and the guayule, seem able to poison the ground around them. A chemical they give off makes sure no other plant can spring up to compete for the little moisture that is available.

The Green Mesquite

Among the many drought survivors, the mesquite of our American deserts is probably one of the hardiest. Mesquites flourish in the driest regions, and their branches are covered with tender green leaves all year long. Yet they do not have a secret method for surviving without water. They need—and they obtain—a constant supply of moisture, and simply go very deep underground to obtain it.

For the first months of its life, the tiny mesquite seedling does little growing above ground. During this period, it is sending its taproot down through the soil toward the water that will keep it alive. Sometimes a root of a mesquite tree grows as deep as 100 feet—the height of a 10-story building. When it finally finds water, the mesquite can put forth leafy shoots and keep them green even during the longest drought. The mesquite is a very hardy plant and is the most widespread type of vegetation in American deserts.

Because of the mesquite's dense growth, sand blown by the wind piles up around it. However, the sand does not smother the plant. The mesquite simply sends new shoots above the

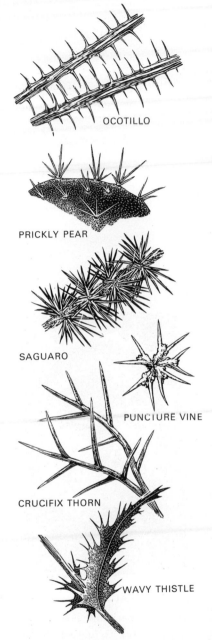

OCOTILLO

PRICKLY PEAR

SAGUARO

PUNCTURE VINE

CRUCIFIX THORN

WAVY THISTLE

THEORIES ON THORNS

Thorns found on so many desert plants long have puzzled botanists. Some believe the thorns were once leaves whose purpose (the making of food) has been taken over by the plants' stems. Other experts think these projections are to give the plants some shade. And there are those who believe thorns are only thorns—a protection plants have evolved to keep from being eaten.

sand pile, and those shoots in turn catch and hold more sand. In time, a solid dune forms around the mesquite. The thick buried limbs within such a dune make one of the world's best firewoods. All over northern Mexico and from southern Texas to Arizona, men dig out these limbs to use as fuel. A man may find half a truckload in a single dune.

The Drought Avoiders

While the drought survivors have developed some fascinating methods to get along in the desert, the other group of plants, the drought avoiders, have some amazing tricks of their own. The drought avoiders make up the largest single group of successful plants that have learned to get along under desert conditions. As mentioned earlier, they are the ones that survive dry periods in the form of seeds. These seeds remain in the ground until conditions are just right for growth. Then they sprout, and the plants flower, bear new seeds and die. The whole cycle usually takes only six to eight weeks. But while they last, these plants, with their bright blossoms, are the most colorful things on the desert.

Over the centuries, desert plant seeds have developed the built-in timing methods for "knowing" just when to sprout in order to produce successful plants. In those deserts which have two rainy seasons each year, some seeds sprout during the first period, others during the second. Each seed seems to "know" which season is best for its own growth.

A scientist made a special study of drought-avoider seeds found in the California desert region. The seeds collected were from various parts of the desert and of many different kinds. Some were the type that sprout after spring rains, and others the kind that sprout after autumn rains.

The scientist who made the tests spread the seed-filled soil he had gathered over layers of sand in flat boxes. Then he treated the various boxes in different ways. He watered some heavily, some lightly. He purposely kept some cool while others were kept heated.

His first discovery was this: simply wetting the thin layer of seed-bearing soil was not enough to make the seeds sprout. Almost none sprouted until he had given them an amount

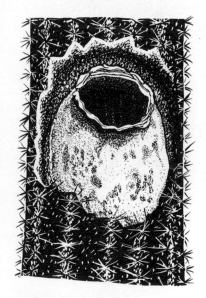

A NEST IN CACTUS

Birds often peck nest holes in the saguaro cactus. To prevent the loss of water from these wounds, the cactus itself produces a protective shell so that the nest hole becomes a dry cavity, like a hollow gourd.

of water equal to at least half an inch of rain—about as much as would fall in a very heavy shower.

He decided that a chemical in the coating of the seed prevents the seed from sprouting until the chemical is dissolved. But a great deal of rain must wash over the seed to remove this chemical.

This chemical which prevents sprouting is called a "growth inhibitor." It serves as a kind of life insurance for seeds. Without a growth inhibitor, the seed might be tricked into sprouting after only a passing shower. Such a shower would not soak the ground sufficiently to provide enough moisture to keep the plant alive during its period of growth, flowering and seed production.

The scientist who conducted these experiments found that seed sprouting also was controlled by soil temperature. The only seeds that sprouted in soil warmed to summer temperatures were those of plants which grow only during the desert summer. The seeds that sprouted in cooler soil were the ones which grow during the desert winter. Soil temperature, in other words, keeps seeds from sprouting until the "right" time for those particular seeds.

The Seed Reserve

The drought avoiders have still another form of survival insurance. During any growing season, even when conditions are ideal, a certain number of seeds will fail to sprout. These remain dormant, or inactive, forming a seed reserve in the soil. Then, even if all the growing plants die before they can produce seeds, a new crop of plants can sprout from the seed supply still in reserve.

Furthermore, the seeds in such a reserve can stay alive for an amazingly long time. A desert area may go without water for several years. Yet the seeds remain alive, waiting to send up shoots when the rain finally falls.

But the seeds of some desert plants require even more than ample water and a certain soil temperature to make them sprout. One example is the mesquite, a plant already described. It is a legume belonging to the family of peas and beans, whose seeds are produced in pods. Mesquite seeds

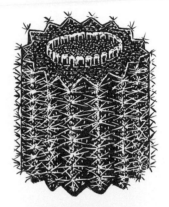

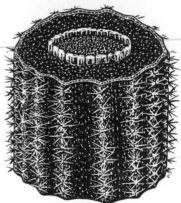

WATER STORAGE

During rainy periods, the saguaro cactus soaks up water in its pulpy stem and grows plump (*bottom*). Then in dry periods, it consumes this stored supply of water, becoming thinner and thinner (*above*).

seldom sprout, even when well watered, unless they first are eaten by some desert animal and have passed through its digestive system. The animal's digestive juices evidently wear away the glassy coat on these seeds, allowing rain water to penetrate, then later start growth.

The seeds of the huge baobab tree, which grows in the Kalahari desert of Africa, are even fussier in their sprouting requirements. They will not sprout until they have passed through the digestive tract of the baboon.

Then there are the seeds of the ironwood and smoke trees, which must be treated roughly before they will grow. Water does not penetrate their hard coats until they are chipped and bruised, usually by being carried violently down a stony wash during a flash flood.

Desert Plants and Insects

In producing seeds, many desert plants are like plants found in other parts of the world: they require the help of insects to pollinate their flowers, and the desert's blooming time is the time when the bees, butterflies and moths appear.

This does not happen accidentally, of course. These insects have been brought out of their pupae or other dormant stages by the same rains that brought out the desert flowers. When the bees appear, they find waiting for them the many flowers whose nectar they collect and without which they would perish. At the same time, other flowers which attract moths and butterflies are beginning to open—and waiting to be pollinated.

It is plain that the timing is vital to both the flowers and the insects. But this timing is also vital to the many insect-eating animals of the desert which rear their young during or after the rainy season. If the insect population failed to appear, the newborn animals would starve.

Thus desert plants provide food for insects, which in turn provide food for insect-eating animals. Desert plants also furnish food for the many animals that live chiefly on seeds.

In other words, these plants—some so frail and others so amazingly tough—support the whole pyramid of life that exists year after year in the deserts of the world.

WHITE, YELLOW AND PURPLE WILD-FLOWER BLOSSOMS BRING VIVID COLOR TO THE BARREN DESERT EARTH

The Desert in Bloom

With the arrival of spring, the great deserts of the American West, which have been brown and dry for perhaps 10 months, suddenly burst into color. Magically the brief rains bring forth carpets of blossoms on the sun-baked soil, and even the spiny stems of the cactuses produce gay, brilliant flowers.

61

DESERT DANDELIONS cover the ground surrounding a weathered butte in the Mojave Desert. As with many desert plants which live only one season, the seeds of the dandelion lie inactive until the spring rains come. Then, all in the space of a few weeks, the plants grow up and produce new seeds before the dry weather begins again.

PURPLE SAND VERBENAS stretch across the Borrego Desert of California. Sticky, moisture-holding substances on their leaves help these verbenas live during periods of dry weather. The shrubs are creosote bushes. Their name comes from their sharp smell, which is like the odor of a preservative used to prevent railroad ties from rotting.

Plants That Store Water

Among the most colorful desert plants are the succulents, whose name comes from a word which means "juicy." They endure dry periods by storing water in the spongy tissues inside their leaves and stems. Often a layer of wax protects them from the drying sun and wind. Many have brightly colored leaves as well as brilliant flowers.

ORANGE FLOWERS, neatly arranged on stems, rise from the center of this aloe plant. Its hoard of water is stored in its thick green leaves. Some aloes grow to 30 feet.

PURPLE LEAVES store water for this African kalanchoe ➤ plant (*right*). In fact, the leaves have so much water that if one falls to the ground, a new plant may sprout from it.

MEXICAN SEDUM has bright orange leaves. Like many other sedums, it is popular as a plant for rock gardens, whose well-drained soil often is as dry as desert soil.

BLUE KLEINIA is a South African succulent that is highly prized by gardeners for its rare foliage color. A waxy coating on the leaves creates the unusual blueness.

HEDGEHOG CACTUS of the Colorado Desert has two-to three-inch blossoms which later become strawberry-flavored fruits. Indians used oil from the seeds in cooking.

BARREL CACTUS, so called for its barrel-like shape, bears its flowers in a circle around the top of its stem. Indians used the curved spines of this plant as fishhooks.

PRICKLY PEAR produces fruits near the end of its flat, paddlelike stem. This cactus is found in more places than any other cactus. It grows wild in all but five states.

GIANT SAGUARO is the largest of the cactuses. It may grow 50 feet tall and live more than 200 years. Its delicate flowers open at night and close the next morning.

Cactuses in Bloom

Most of us, when we think about cactuses, think of thorns and spines and getting our fingers stuck. But when cactuses are in bloom, they are among the most beautiful plants in the desert. The flowers of several cactuses are shown on these pages. They range in color from snowy white to fiery red. And they range in size from tiny blossoms to flowers bigger than a saucer. Many of these cactuses also bear fruits.

One of the most famous desert plants is the night-blooming cereus. This plant produces a single flower once each year. It blooms at night and fades the next morning.

CANDY CACTUS is a bright-blossomed, barrel-shaped ➤ Arizona plant (right). Sugar mixed with the meaty center of the stem makes a confection known as "cactus candy."

This fierce-looking horned lizard, only three inches long, is actually harmless and makes a good pet. Its horns are not used for fighting, but they make this fellow a spiny meal. Its diet is made up mostly of ants

4

Animals That Live in the Desert

It is high noon on a summer day and you are standing alone in the middle of the Mojave (Mo-*hah*-veh) Desert. The temperature of the air is close to 110° —but the sand underfoot is a searing 160° . The only sound is the sighing hiss of the wind blowing through the mesquite bushes. You feel the hot breath of the wind blowing against your cheek. It actually seems almost as if you were standing in front of an open oven door.

But more than anything, you are struck by the feeling of being alone. Except for the plants, you are the only living thing anywhere, so far as you can see.

That is the way it seems. Yet in reality, in this silent, sun-scorched place there are thousands of animals. All about you there are insects, spiders, snakes, rabbits, bats, birds, lizards, rats and foxes—all going about their business. And their business, of course, is *living* in this unfriendly place.

Yet to these animals the desert is not unfriendly. For them it is the only way of life they have ever known. They might even die outside the desert.

Like desert plants, these creatures have found ways to get

along under desert conditions of little water and much heat.

Unlike desert plants, which have two ways of surviving under these conditions, desert animals have developed many ways of living in the desert. For example, some desert animals have to drink water twice a day, but there are others that may never drink water at all.

Animals Avoid Heat

To understand how animals get along in the desert, you must first understand an important fact: Most desert creatures are not heat lovers. They cannot take much higher temperatures than human beings can. A body temperature of only 101° may kill a snake, and lizards collapse when their body temperatures get up around 105°.

How, then, do they survive the heat of the desert floor, which may go as high as 180°? The fact is that they could not. Any lizard on earth would die in a few minutes if it were foolish enough to expose itself to such heat.

Most desert animals never even appear during the day, and those that do spend most of their time in the shade. The point here is that all desert creatures must have some kind of shelter from the sun.

Take the mammals, for example. In forest regions, only about one out of every 16 kinds of mammals lives in a burrow. But almost three quarters of the kinds of mammals that live in deserts have burrows.

These shelters vary a great deal. One animal may find all the protection it needs in the shade of a mesquite bush or an overhanging rock. And some birds nest in a hole bored in the stem of a cactus.

But probably the best kind of shelter is found in a burrow dug under the sand of the desert floor. Sand or earth is a wonderful protection against both heat and cold.

Studies have shown that an animal's burrow only four inches underground is 31° cooler than the temperature on the surface of the ground. Of course the deeper a burrow is, the cooler it will be. In the desert, the sun often cooks the ground to a temperature of 150° or more. But in a burrow 18 inches underground the temperature will be a cool 61°.

That is 89° cooler than the temperature on the surface of the ground.

And so we find a great many desert creatures living underground much of the time. Some snakes and lizards probably have one of the simplest kinds of shelter from the sun. They just dig themselves down into the sand to escape the daytime heat. And in order to do this, some desert reptiles have a special breathing arrangement. Their noses are formed in such a way that they can get air without choking on the sand in which they are buried.

As we have already mentioned, most desert mammals also escape the heat in burrows. Indeed some, like gophers, almost never go above ground since their food is made up mainly of roots and bulbs which are dug from underground. Another burrow builder is the small kangaroo rat—which is neither a kangaroo nor a rat, though it looks like both. Groups of kangaroo rats build large community burrows in which they escape the heat. The entrances are plugged with a kind of stopper made out of dirt. Snug in its burrow with the stopper in place, the kangaroo rat even has pleasantly damp air to breathe. The dampness comes from the moisture of its own breath.

Desert insects also live underground in burrows. The harvester ants live in burrows deeper than 15 feet underground, where the temperature is pleasantly cool. The harvester ants never go out in the heat of the day.

But not all burrows are underground. Some pack rats, for example, build "stick houses," four or five feet high, while others pile the entrances of their burrows with pieces of cholla—the most prickly cactus in the desert.

Animals Take Over Burrows

And while desert birds don't actually dig burrows, a few of them live in them. The burrowing owl is one. It escapes the heat of the day by crawling into a burrow dug by some other animal. Another owl that relies on others for its home is the tiny elf owl, only six inches long. The elf owl moves into old nests pecked into large cactuses by woodpeckers. These nests are usually on the east or northeast side of the

A DIGGING TOAD

The spadefoot toad digs a burrow backward into the ground (*above*) at the start of a drought. The horny, rounded spur on the bottom of its hind foot (*below*) is its "spade." This toad can lie dormant underground for months. The toad leaves its burrow when fresh rains come.

plants, where they will be shaded from the hot glare of the afternoon sun.

It is fairly common in the desert for one animal to take over a burrow built by another animal. Rattlesnakes are famous for moving in where they are not wanted. The trouble is that once a rattlesnake has moved in, it's no easy matter to get rid of it. Just to go in and pull the snake out would not be very wise.

Prairie Dogs and Rattlesnakes

But the perky little prairie dogs of the grassy plains regions have solved this problem. Prairie dogs, which look something like overgrown chipmunks, are champion burrow builders and dig whole "towns" underground.

When a rattlesnake decides to set up housekeeping in a prairie-dog burrow, there isn't much the prairie dogs can do to prevent it. But they can make the rattlesnake awfully sorry about the home it decided to take over. The prairie dogs wait until the snake is deep inside the burrow. Then they begin busily digging and shoveling dirt and sand into the entrance hole.

When the hole is filled up, the prairie dogs pack this earthen plug down very firmly. The sun does the rest. Soon the dirt plug is baked hard and dry, and the burrow is sealed up—with the rattlesnake inside. After that it is simply a matter of waiting for the rattlesnake to die—from a lack of air, thirst or starvation.

As we know, the hottest part of the desert is the surface of the ground. This is just like sand at a beach. You can burn your feet walking across a beach on a hot summer's day. Some desert lizards have overcome this problem. They have long thin legs which keep their bodies well off the ground. Grasshoppers also manage to move about the desert floor without touching it, except with their sticklike legs.

Thus, desert creatures avoid the deadly heat of midday. Recent studies suggest that some desert animals are born with special temperature-sensitive organs that warn them when to seek shelter from the hot sun. The spiny lizard of California is one. It has a kind of sightless "eye" in the center

THE GILA MONSTER

This lizard, the only poisonous one in the United States, is a sluggish creature. It feeds on eggs or small animals. It grabs its prey between powerful jaws, then hangs on and chews. Poison from glands in its bottom jaw flows into the wound through grooved teeth. Its bite is almost never fatal to human beings.

of its forehead which tells it when to get into the shade.

Naturally, if escape from the heat were the only problem facing desert animals, life for them would be quite simple. They could just stay in their shelters and all would be well. But of course they cannot. They must go out to find food and water.

In this regard, the creatures of the desert generally fall into two groups: There are animals which are active during the day, and those which are active only at night.

As the sun comes up in the desert, the early risers begin to stir. Among them are most of the birds, including the insect eaters and the seed eaters. There are also vultures, which feed on dead animals. And there are hawks and the strutting road runners—birds which do a great deal more running than flying.

Reptiles—snakes and lizards—are one of the chief items in the diet of hawks and road runners. The road runners look for them on the ground while the hawks circle high overhead in the hope of spotting a meal.

But as the morning wears on, the temperature begins to rise, and soon it is too hot for the birds. They must seek shelter. The heat of the day also drives the jack rabbits into their burrows. The same is true of many insects. The harvester ants are now safe underground.

As noon approaches, a kind of quiet falls over the desert. Even the reptiles have found a patch of shade to escape the terrible heat of the sun.

The Coming of Night

But as the afternoon grows older and the temperature begins to fall, the birds and rabbits appear once again. There is still time for an evening meal, and they are busy looking for food.

Finally the sun is down and evening comes. Almost at once the temperature begins to drop. By now the lizards are snugly bedded down and the bull snakes are fast asleep. The road runners are back in their nests.

But for every animal that is going to sleep, at least two others seem to be waking up—for night is the period of greatest animal activity in the desert. The night-flying owls blink their huge yellow eyes and stretch their wings. And from a nearby cave in the face of a cliff comes a strange muffled sound. It is the beating of thousands of wings as the desert bats pour out into the night to begin their hungry search for insects. By morning, when the bats return to the cave, each one will have consumed about half its own weight in insects.

A Busy Time

Down on the desert floor, where the temperature is now quite cool, an assortment of rodents has appeared, along with coyotes, bobcats, skunks and badgers.

Now the stars are out. The air is cool, and the desert floor, so burning hot a few hours before, is almost cold. It seems to be a scene of peace and stillness.

But the truth is that this is the busiest period of all in the desert—and anything but peaceful.

Night is the time when the mammals of the desert are active. On American deserts, these animals range in size from the tiny pocket mouse, which is not much bigger than a person's finger, to the doglike coyote.

The badger is busy with its powerful front paws, digging a lizard out of its burrow. The kit fox is stalking a pack rat, unaware that it is being stalked, in turn, by a bobcat.

Overhead the horned owl flies along, looking for a victim. It has thick, soft feathers which enable it to fly without making the faintest sound. Down on the ground, a rattlesnake surprises a little kangaroo rat. But the snake doesn't get its meal. The kangaroo rat kicks sand into the snake's eyes and escapes.

All night long this busy activity goes on. But finally the first light of the approaching morning brightens the sky. The night creatures return to their burrows or their nests.

So we see that all this animal activity follows a regular pattern every day. But there are other patterns which cover longer periods. These are the seasonal patterns, which may last for several months. There are also yearly patterns. The best way to understand this is to study a few examples.

Now you will remember that most deserts have different seasons at different times of the year. There are the long, hot periods of drought when plant food is very scarce. And then come the periods of brief and usually heavy rain, after which all desert plant life blooms.

These changes of climate also account for the seasonal cycles of behavior in many desert animals. Take, for example, the spadefoot toad. This little fellow gets its name from a small shovel-like growth on its hind feet, which the toad uses to dig itself into the ground.

During most of the year—sometimes as long as nine months—the spadefoot toad is buried underground, where it is sleeping. It remains in this state until a cloudburst of rain falls in the spring.

As the rain soaks down into the ground, the toad wakes up, digs itself out and heads for the nearest puddle to lay its eggs. It takes only a day or two for the eggs to hatch into tadpoles. Within a month these tadpoles have become toads. As the weather turns hotter and the mud flats begin to dry, the spadefoot toads dig themselves down into the mud to begin their long sleep.

This is the yearly pattern of the spadefoot toad—three months of active life, when there is water around, followed by a long sleep of nine months.

Some 25-Year-Old Eggs

Some desert creatures have adjusted to even longer periods of waiting for the life-giving rains to come. Probably the best example is the fresh-water shrimp found in our own Western deserts. These are really very tiny shrimp, only about as big as a honeybee.

These shrimp hatch from eggs. But shrimp are creatures which live in water. Without water, the eggs will not hatch. And so these eggs may lie on the dried-up desert mud flats year after year, waiting until there is enough rain to allow them to hatch. When the rains come, the mud flats are turned into shallow lakes, alive with shrimp.

These shrimp may live only a short while, but that is long enough for them to lay eggs. How long it will be before

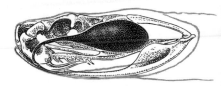

A RATTLER'S FANGS

The fangs of a rattler are attached to the snake's upper jaw, which is flexible. They can fold inward when the snake's mouth is closed (*above*). When the mouth is opened in an attack, these fangs straighten out (*below*). The fangs are hollow, and the rattlesnake's poison is injected through them from the balloonlike venom glands (shaded in brown).

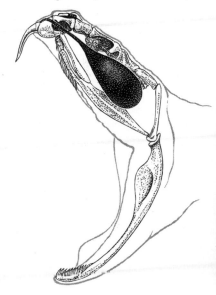

the eggs hatch depends mostly on the rain that falls on the region. There was one place in the Mojave Desert where 25 years went by without rain. But finally there was a huge rainstorm—and shrimp eggs a quarter of a century old suddenly hatched. However, a waiting period that long is very unusual indeed.

The Birds and the Seasons

The seasonal behavior of most desert animals is much more regular than this. Birds are a good example. There are many kinds of birds which appear in the deserts only when conditions there are right. Thus the number of birds found in deserts is least during the cold winters and hot summers. In the spring, however, the bird population in the deserts increases greatly.

After the brief rains of early spring, the plants begin to bloom. There are flowers that provide food for such birds as hummingbirds, which sip the nectar. Later these plants will produce seeds—the food of the seed-eating birds. And of course spring is the time when most of the desert insects hatch. These insects are the food for most young birds in the desert. So it is very important that young birds hatch at a time when the greatest number of insects are about. To make certain this happens, the adult birds must lay their eggs at just the right time.

Over thousands of years, birds have developed a sense of timing about when to lay their eggs. It is all a part of their seasonal cycle, and usually birds lay eggs every year. Some sort of signal tells them exactly when the right time has come. They find a mate, build a nest, lay their eggs—and the young birds are hatched just as the desert insects are beginning to appear.

But this is not true of all desert birds. Some birds may live in pairs for several years of poor rainfall but never build a nest or lay eggs. Then a heavy rainstorm begins to drench the area. Almost at once these birds will begin to build themselves a nest, and later they will lay eggs. It is almost as if the rain has told them that there will be insects and growing plants. This means that there will be plenty of food for all.

While on the subject of desert birds, let's look at the vultures. It would be hard to imagine uglier birds. They are quite large and often black, with bald heads and hooked beaks. Vultures have become a symbol of deserts, probably because they are thought of in connection with death.

This is because vultures eat the flesh of dead animals. With their huge wingspread, they circle high overhead, riding the rising currents of hot air. Vultures have incredibly good vision, and they can spot the body of a dead animal from miles away. More than that, they seem able to spot an animal that is going to die. Then the vultures circle overhead, following the animal as it moves along and waiting for it to die.

In the days of the early pioneers, who struggled across the desert in covered wagons, one of the most alarming things was the sight of vultures in the sky. Unfortunately, too often the instinct of the vultures proved right, and the pioneers died on the trail.

For this reason, vultures have always had a bad name. They were a symbol of bad luck. It was as if they were going to harm desert travelers. But the truth is that vultures themselves—even though they are so large—are both weak and timid. Because vultures are so weak and timid, they are unable to kill prey of their own. They have to rely on food that is already dead.

How Animals Protect Themselves

Nearly all desert animals face the problem of being hunted by other animals. While no animal has a sure method of protecting itself, many have developed some curious methods of defenses.

One of the most curious is used by lizards. With the one exception of the Gila (*hee*-lah) monster, all desert lizards have the ability to lose their tails. This means that if a lizard is grabbed by the tail, the tail simply breaks off, and the lizard escapes. The lizard suffers no harm, and eventually grows a new tail to replace the one it lost.

And one lizard, the chuckwalla, has an added trick for protecting itself. When an enemy appears, the chuckwalla

A DESERT JUMPER

The jerboas of Africa and Asia are very similar, although unrelated, to the American kangaroo rat. Both have a long tufted tail for balance, whiskered feet for jumping on the soft sand, and long, powerful hind legs. The legs can boost the jerboa's tiny six-inch body in tremendous leaps, which may carry it six feet.

crawls into a rock crevice, then sucks in air. This makes the chuckwalla swell up and wedges it between the rocks.

Among the desert birds, the little burrowing owl, which is only 10 inches tall, does its best to look frightening whenever it is threatened. It ruffs out its wings and puffs out its chest in order to make itself look bigger than it is. At the same time, the burrowing owl squawks at its attacker, making a very fierce noise.

The bird with one of the safest nests in the desert is the cactus wren. It builds its nest in the prickly cholla cactus.

During the nesting season, poorwills will sometimes pretend to be injured after their young have been hatched. They hold one wing as if it were broken, and limp across the ground. The purpose of this is to lure an attacker away from the young birds in the nest.

A great many desert animals rely for protection on the fact that they are hard to see. Their colors blend in with those of the land around them. One of the best examples of this is the little horned lizard, which is colored in shades of brown and gray so that it becomes very nearly invisible against the ground.

The fringe-toed sand lizard goes a step further. At the approach of danger, it does a kind of disappearing act by "swimming" down into the sand. After a few wriggles of its body, there is hardly a mark on the surface to show its hiding place.

The Puzzle of the Skunk

The spotted skunk of the desert has developed a puzzling trick to confuse its enemies. This animal is smaller and livelier than the striped kind that everybody is so careful to avoid. Just like its big cousin, the spotted skunk is equipped with an evil-smelling liquid.

But this seems to be used only in cases of great emergency. When a little everyday threat appears, the spotted skunk does a handstand on its front paws. Exactly why a little skunk doing a handstand should be a less attractive meal than a little skunk standing on all fours remains one of the mysteries of the desert.

BRIGHT EYES THAT SEE IN THE DARK BELONG TO A BANDED GECKO, A SMALL LIZARD THAT HUNTS AT NIGHT

Survival in the Desert

American deserts look like poor places for animals to live in. Water is scarce here and plants are few. There is little shade from the scorching sun. Yet our deserts support some five thousand different kinds of reptiles, birds, mammals and insects that have adapted well to the hot regions they inhabit.

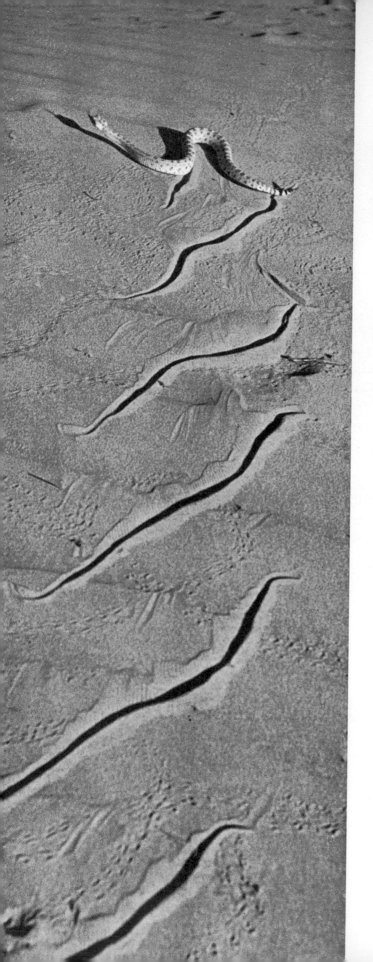

A CHUCKWALLA LIZARD CAN PUFF ITSELF UP WITH

Adaptations of Desert Reptiles

Reptiles have adapted to their desert home in various unusual ways. To avoid attack, the shovel-nosed ground snake swims invisibly beneath the sand. The horned lizard is difficult to see against the sand. But heat is the biggest problem. Reptiles must move from sun to shade because their temperature depends on the temperature of their surroundings. In heat higher than 105°, most reptiles show signs of great strain.

A SIDEWINDER RATTLER travels across the loose sand (*left*) by looping its body sideways, head first, in a flowing S curve. Its track looks like a parallel series of gashes.

AIR UNTIL IT BECOMES SO TIGHTLY WEDGED IN A ROCK CREVICE THAT ITS ENEMIES CANNOT PULL IT OUT

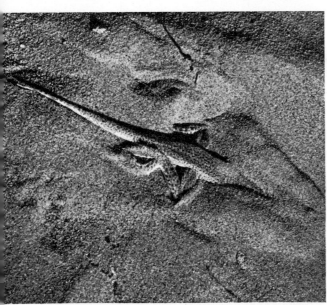

A FRINGE-TOED SAND LIZARD uses loose sand as a means of hiding from enemies. When threatened, it dives in head first *(above, left)* and "swims" out of sight in sec-onds *(right)*. Specially constructed fringes on its toes make the vanishing act possible. A built-in sand trap in its nose allows it to breathe under sand without choking.

81

A BUTTON-EYED KANGAROO RAT STANDS POISED AND ALERT. ITS CHEEK POUCHES ARE STUFFED WITH SEEDS

WITH TAILS FLYING, two angry kangaroo rats begin a free-for-all near their burrows. Balancing with their tails, the rats can flick a quarter-turn in the middle of a jump.

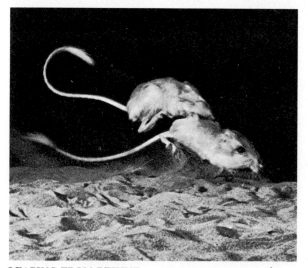

LEAPING FROM BEHIND, one rat prepares to strike at the other in mid-air with its strong hind feet. With a solid blow, a rat sometimes can kick another several feet.

The Remarkable Kangaroo Rat

Cranky, clever and curious, the kangaroo rat is the wonder of the American desert. Barely two inches tall, the kangaroo rat has long hind legs, big feet and a tufted tail three times as long as its body. All these help it to do one thing: to hop.

The kangaroo rat can travel 17 feet per second. It can flip high in the air and, using its tail as a rudder, make right-angle turns in mid-flight. Though quarrelsome little creatures, kangaroo rats live in large community burrows about two feet under the ground.

Hawks, snakes, bobcats and kit foxes all feed on the kangaroo rat. Its flesh provides them with water as well as food—even though the kangaroo rat itself may live a lifetime without ever drinking water. It gets all the moisture it requires from its food. And it conserves water by sealing itself into its cool burrow during the day.

KICKING SAND at its opponent's eyes is a favorite and effective battle tactic. Kangaroo rats also kick up sand to ward off larger attackers, such as snakes and kit foxes.

LEAPING HIGH, a rat avoids its opponent with a foot-and-a-half leap. Scuffles like this one usually come to an end when one rat has had enough and hops away.

83

A PLUMP PACK RAT picks its way carefully over the desert's most prickly cactus, the cholla. The rats are a favorite food of the kit fox and pile up cholla stems to protect the entrances to their burrows. These are usually storehouses for a variety of odds and ends the rats are fond of collecting. This habit accounts for their name.

A LEAN KIT FOX crouches in wait for prey. The kit fox is well equipped for hunting at night in the desert. It listens with huge ears for the scampering of desert rodents. The kit fox is very swift over short distances and runs down its victim in brief, furious dashes. After the kill it returns to its burrow to eat its meal at leisure.

A WHITE-WINGED DOVE spreads its wings for a landing beside its mate. Unlike many birds, these summertime visitors to the American Southwest seem to like heat.

These birds must drink at least once a day, and an old Indian trick for finding water in the desert is to follow the straight-line flight of doves to their source of water.

CLUTCHING AN INSECT, a red-topped Gila woodpecker climbs to its nest hole in a saguaro. The hole pecked into the cactus pulp dries on the inside, making a fine nest.

Problems for Desert Birds

Birds have not made much of an adaption to desert living, and their bodies have changed little to protect them from the heat. Only the burrowing owl has learned to go underground. Other birds cool off by losing water through their lungs. Most birds replace this lost water from their food, but the seedeaters must drink daily.

NESTING IN THORNS, a road runner sits on its eggs in a tangle of twigs. The parent birds take turns sitting on the nest between trips to hunt for snakes and lizards.

GUARDING ITS HOME, an elf owl peers out from an old nest hole made by a Gila woodpecker. The elf owl is only six inches high—the smallest owl in the world.

87

BARE, BRIGHT HEAD of a turkey vulture hunches down into its feathers. Vultures live on dead flesh and soar high above the desert for hours searching for carcasses.

BARE, BONY BODIES of hairless young bats (*right*) hang → in the depths of a mine shaft. They sleep during the hot desert day, then swarm out at night to hunt for insects.

A GHOSTLY WOLF SPIDER moves out of its den to go hunting. Light shines in six of its eight eyes. Two of its eyes are on top of its head. The wolf spider does not spin a web but roams the desert on foot. Scarcely one inch across, this spider catches its passing insect prey by jumping from a small mound next to its burrow.

90

A **FEMALE SCORPION** heads for cover with its brood of babies clinging to its back. The scorpion's sting is widely feared but is dangerous in only two out of 12 species.

Scorpions, Spiders and Others

An important link in the desert food chain is its population of insects, which thrive by the millions. Birds, bats and many reptiles are dependent on them for food. These insects are also essential to the spiders and their relations, the scorpions and solpugids, which look like insects but are not. These powerful hunters often will eat their own weight in insects daily. By so doing, they help to keep the desert's insect population within bounds. But spiders are themselves food for many animals. Spiders consist of over 80 per cent liquid. An owl feeding on them can live for a season without water.

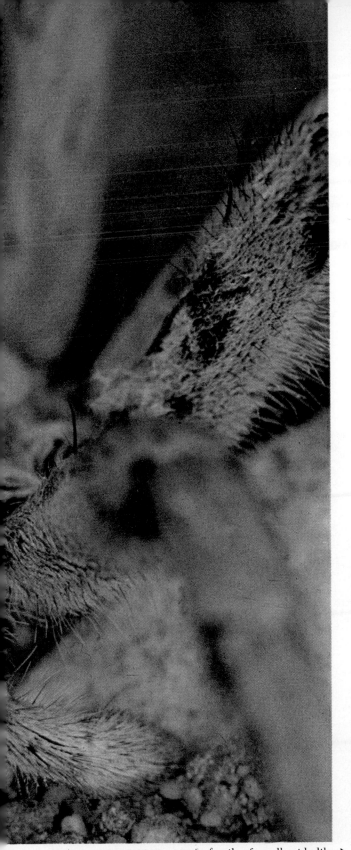

A **HUNGRY SOLPUGID,** one of a family of small spiderlike➤ creatures, sinks sharp fangs into a cricket *(right)*. It drains its victim's body juices, leaving only an empty husk.

The Vital Water Hole

The center of much desert animal life is the water hole. This precious water source sometimes can be found in a hollow where underground water seeps to the surface. It attracts many animals in the course of a day. At evening, during a dry spell, it may be crowded with many different species, all replacing the water they lost that day. Even natural enemies do not fight here, but wait their turn. First come mule deer, then coyotes, badgers, weasels, foxes. But a herd of peccaries or a skunk may interrupt the order. When the larger animals are finished, the smaller ones get their turn.

SHY MULE DEER start up from a water hole. Their long ears are spread to detect any sound. Mule deer drink at least once a day and feed on plants that grow near water.

THIRSTY PECCARIES gather for a drink. They also obtain water by digging up the roots of cactuses and other plants. They are North America's only native wild pigs.

HUNGRY BADGER gnaws on a desert iguana *(right)*. ➤ The badger is a powerful digger, often plowing deep into the earth and catching rodents in their burrows.

92

Camels drink at a desert watering trough. Camels may go for months without water if they can feed on green plants. They can work a week without food or drink by living off the fat stored within their humps.

5

Water: The Endless Problem

There is an old saying that you never appreciate anything until you have to do without it. That is the way most of us feel about water. There is so much water around that we hardly ever think about it. Our country is bounded by oceans on three sides. It is dotted with lakes and cut by thousands of rivers, streams and brooks.

For this reason we find it difficult to understand how hard it must be for the people who live in deserts. Often these people have to struggle just to get enough water to stay alive—and many of them may go for years without enough water even to take a bath.

Just imagine, if you can, what water means to the Bushman tribes who live in the barren Kalahari desert, which is in southern Africa. In order to get enough water just for drinking and for cooking, the Bushmen actually have to suck it out of the ground.

To do this, the Bushmen dig what they call a "sucking well," a hole in the sand a foot or two deep. The bottom of the hole is filled with dry grass, and a hollow reed is stuck in the center. Then the hole is filled up again with sand.

After a while a Bushman bends over and begins to suck on the hollow reed. If he is lucky, he may begin to suck up the few drops of water that have seeped into the hole from underground. The grass in the bottom of the hole keeps the sand from getting in his mouth.

The Bushman's job is to get enough water to fill up an empty ostrich egg so that others in the tribe may have a drink, too. So the Bushman continues to suck on the reed, and whatever water he gets he spits into the empty ostrich egg. Sometimes it takes hours of sucking to fill up the shell, and by the time he has completed the job, the Bushman may have sore cheeks.

Digging Desert Wells

These "sucking wells" tell us two things: They show us the hard time that some desert people have in getting the water they need. But more than that, they show us that water in the desert often is obtained from underground. Even in the Sahara, there are always places where there is water underground—though you may have to dig very deep to get it, sometimes through many layers of rock.

Some desert water wells occur naturally, where water has simply bubbled up to the surface. But more often these wells have been dug by men. The task is one of the most colorful sights in the Sahara.

The methods used are very old. The boss in charge of the operation assembles his men, each one with his own hoe. Off to one side there are several drummers and usually one man with a native flute. At a signal from the foreman, the musicians begin to play.

"Who's a husky worker?" sings the foreman in time with the music.

"That's us!" the workers shout.

"Who digs the deepest trench?" the foreman sings.

"That's us!" the workers reply.

Over and over again the song is repeated. And every time the workers shout "That's us!" they bring their hoes down to scoop out some more dirt.

Once a well has been dug in the desert, the next problem

is to keep it from filling back up with sand. At one time this job was done by men who earned their living removing sand which might clog the wells. It was hard work and also dangerous because these well diggers were forced to dive deep down into the cold waters to get at the sand.

There was a little ceremony to the way they worked. First they plugged their ears with wax as a protection against the water pressure. Then they built a small fire close by the well in order to warm themselves before plunging into the icy water. When they were warm enough, each diver recited a prayer asking that he be kept safe.

Finally it was time to dive. Each well digger took several very deep breaths—then took one last long breath and dived under the surface of the water in the well.

These well diggers were famous for the length of time they could hold their breath underwater—sometimes as long as five minutes. During all that time, they were busy scooping sand into a small basket.

When a man's basket was full, he came back up to the surface. Usually he was shivering from the cold and had to warm himself by the fire again.

The depth of water in a well will vary, of course, but it frequently will be 20 feet or more. Working in the cold, deep water was so tiring that a well digger might be able to make only two dives a day. This meant that in the course of a day's work, each well digger removed only about as much sand as would fill a shoebox. Obviously, cleaning out a desert well was a slow process.

A Look at an Oasis

The most famous source of water found in the deserts is the oasis. The word was first used by the ancient Greeks. It means "fertile land." And that is what an oasis is—a garden in the desert.

Stories about the desert almost always picture an oasis as a sort of quiet little park. There is a small grove of palm trees, with a well or pond in the center. But the truth is that a real oasis seldom looks like that.

First, most oases are much larger than you would think.

While some are no bigger than a small orchard, many cover several square miles. In addition, an oasis is most often the location of a village, town or city.

As you approach an oasis you first see a mass of dark green, which stands out in contrast to the yellow sand all around. This green you see is the tops of palm trees, and as you get closer you see the graceful curves of their trunks.

Drawing nearer still, you see that this precious watered land is not like a park at all. Instead, every available foot is given to the growing of crops. The tall date palm trees are planted in neat rows, with each tree about 16 feet from its nearest neighbor.

Beneath the trees are square patches of land which have been marked off into garden plots that are planted with vegetables or wheat.

The Life-giving Date Palms

Unlike the storybook version of an oasis, there are no houses or buildings in the center. No desert dweller would think of using food-producing land to put a building on. Instead the buildings are all clustered at the edge of the oasis where no crops will grow. These villages of flat-topped mud houses are usually built up two or more stories in order to take up the least amount of usable ground.

When most people think about an oasis, the picture of date palm trees comes to mind. We have no single food which even compares in importance to dates for the people of the Sahara. Dates are often eaten at every meal—and frequently they are the main course.

But the use of dates does not end with eating the fruit. The pits inside the dates also have many uses. Sometimes they are roasted and used as a substitute for coffee. Other times they are ground up to make date flour, which goes into the making of pancakes. Sometimes the pits are squeezed to obtain oil which is then used for cooking. And even the mashed-up pits have a use. Caravans carry sacks of them, and when no camel food is available, the crushed pits are mixed with water and fed to the camels.

In addition, the juice of dates is made into "date honey."

A HUMP OF NOURISHMENT

The camel's hump consists mostly of a fat produced when food and water are plentiful. When there is very little to eat or drink, this fat is consumed in place of food. The camel's digestive system turns the fat into juices and body fluids. A camel can work efficiently without water, but it will grow lean in the process *(top)*. When water is made available, a camel often will drink more than 25 gallons in the space of 10 minutes. Its body then fills out and the camel returns to its normally plump shape *(bottom)*.

The sap of the tree itself is served as a sweet drink. The trunk of the tree provides fire logs, wood for building and fiber for sacks, ropes and sandals.

It is not hard to see how important date palm trees are to many people who live in the Sahara. Now let us see how these people get their palm trees to grow.

A desert dweller who plants a grove of palm trees must be a patient fellow, prepared to do a lot of work. First of all, he must see to it that there is a reliable source of water which will last for years to come. This will take close attention because desert wells, as we have seen, have a habit of filling up with sand.

Next, the farmer must plant his young trees and watch over them year after year. They must be fertilized and protected during periods of bad weather. He must dig irrigation ditches around the trees to water them. Then finally, after 20 long years of work and waiting, the date palm farmer can expect a full crop of fruit.

But there are rewards for all this trouble. A good-sized date palm will produce up to 300 pounds of dates a year. Not only that, but if a date palm tree is given a good supply of water, it will keep on producing dates for as long as 200 years. That means that the great-great-great-great-grandson of the farmer who first planted the trees will still be harvesting the dates.

The Reason for an Oasis

A natural oasis does not come about by accident. Shifts in the earth's surface produce cracks through which water from underground may bubble to the surface.

In the Sahara, one such crack is particularly interesting. It is in the western part of the desert and it stretches for a distance of 745 miles. Along this huge crack, there is one natural oasis after another, stretching like a green ribbon of vegetation through the heart of the desert. Over the years, this long string of oases has come to be known as the "Street of Palms."

While the most reliable supplies of water in the desert come from underground, deserts also get water in the form

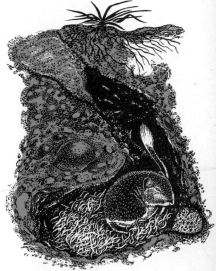

A COZY BURROW

A kangaroo rat survives dry spells by hiding in a cool underground burrow during the day. It seals the opening with a plug of earth *(top),* which keeps out the heat and keeps in the moisture of the rat's breath. In this way the burrow and the kangaroo rat's stockpile of seeds *(lower right)* remain moist. The rat ventures out to feed only at night.

of precipitation. This is a word used to mean water in any form which falls to the earth from the clouds. The most common form of precipitation, of course, is rain. But precipitation also refers to snow, hail and sleet.

The idea that precipitation comes to the desert only in the form of violent cloudbursts is not so. True enough, such downpours are probably the most frequent type of precipitation in the desert. But there are others.

Snow is not uncommon in deserts at certain seasons—and it frequently snows in the Sahara at high altitudes. At the height of summer, the parched Gobi desert of Mongolia is sometimes blanketed by ice which has fallen during a hailstorm. As we learned in Chapter Two, the deserts of Peru are almost always cloaked in fog, although weathermen do not consider fog precipitation. On rare occasions deserts may have long periods of wet, gloomy weather.

Man and Water

So far we have talked about how water is obtained in deserts. Now let us look at how animals make use of this water (or learn to get along without it) under very dry conditions. And let us begin with man.

As an animal, man is poorly equipped for desert life. Take away a man's water supply and put him out in a desert on the morning of a hot summer day. At first he will feel little discomfort. But after an hour, he will be very thirsty because his body will have perspired away a quart of water.

By midafternoon, he will have perspired so much that he will have lost 12 to 18 pounds. He will also have begun to feel weak. If the desert temperature reaches 120°, he may be dead by night. But if the temperature does not rise over 110° in the shade, the man might live through one more day.

To understand all this, you must understand a little of how the human body works. Even if a person is sitting perfectly still in the shade, his body is producing a considerable amount of heat. His heart is beating. His stomach is digesting food. And all the other body processes are going on. All this creates heat inside the body.

Now, in order to keep the body at what is called our

"normal" temperature, this heat is carried to the surface of the body—the skin. To rid the body of this heat, the sweat glands in the skin give off moisture in the form of perspiration. The sweat is then evaporated by the heat of the skin and this evaporation carries the heat away from the body.

Under the conditions of fierce heat found in deserts, the human body is put under a terrible strain. It must get rid of its inside heat when the temperature outside is, let us say, 115°. That is about 16° hotter than the "normal" temperature of the human body.

In such a situation, the body's two million little sweat glands have to work so hard that they begin to heat up themselves. This overheating creates a fever, which raises a person's temperature even more.

The human body can keep up this struggle only for a short time. After that, the body's whole cooling system begins to wear out. A person provided with all the water he can drink will probably last only a week under desert conditions.

The killing heat of the desert is an ever-present threat to other animals, too. We have already seen that lizards and birds collapse if their body temperatures climb much above 100°. And the mammals which live in deserts can survive only slightly higher temperatures.

Animals and Water

There are two ways desert animals manage to live with the heat: They can escape it by going underground, or they can keep their bodies cool with water. Those animals which use water cool themselves by means of evaporation—the same as man does when he sweats. But most animals do not sweat through their skin as human beings do. They evaporate water in their lungs or in their mouths.

The most familiar example of an animal which evaporates water from its lungs is the dog. When a dog gets hot, it pants—and by breathing more air, it also evaporates more water. Other animals which cool themselves by panting away water are birds, reptiles, foxes and coyotes.

Two animals which get rid of heat by evaporating water in their mouths are found in Australia. They are the cuddly

A DESERT HIBERNATOR

The poorwill hibernates during the winter months. In the fall the bird eats a great deal and grows plump with stored fat. When the desert becomes cold, the poorwill sinks into a state of dormancy for several weeks. It is quite safe on the desert floor because its feathers blend with the color of the ground.

koala bear and the wallaby, a relative of the kangaroo. Whenever the koala gets overheated, water flows into its mouth. The hotter the animal gets, the more saliva it produces. In really hot weather, the koala licks its front legs to get rid of the extra water which collects in its mouth. And when a wallaby gets hot, it licks itself all over.

There are few animals which get rid of heat by sweating through the skin as man does. Among these are horses and rabbits. The rabbit has enormous ears. These help the rabbit to hear better. But they are equally important in providing a large skin area where sweat can evaporate.

Animal "Water Factories"

But no matter how an animal loses water to keep cool, it must obtain the water in the first place. There are three methods. The first, naturally, is by drinking water. Also, water may be obtained by eating certain foods. The third method is a special one used by certain desert animals— especially the camel. The camel is able to produce what is called "metabolic water" inside its own body.

For centuries, people believed the camel had a reserve water tank somewhere inside its body. But the truth is that the camel has no secret tanks of water. What the camel does have is a large store of fat in its hump. It also has the ability to change this fat into body juices.

During the long, dry periods when a camel goes without drinking water, it is simply getting needed energy and body juices from this reserve of fat in its hump. The juices are referred to as "metabolic water." A camel which has been on a week's journey across the desert loses a great deal of weight because it is using up its stored fat.

But at the end of the journey, the camel must be given water. It will then drink as much as 25 gallons in the space of 10 minutes. In this way, the camel replaces the weight lost from its hump.

And so we see that even a camel needs water. The point to remember here is this: There are many substances necessary to life. But living things—and that includes all plants and all animals—share the need for water.

THE TORTOISE CARRIES ITS OWN WATER SUPPLY. SACS UNDER ITS SHELL MAY HOLD ALMOST A PINT OF WATER

Life-giving Water

Desert life is adjusted to the availability of water. Seeds and eggs may wait years for the life-giving rains to come. When they do come, these rains are sometimes so violent they kill the very plants and creatures which endured so long without water. Also, there are rains which never reach the ground.

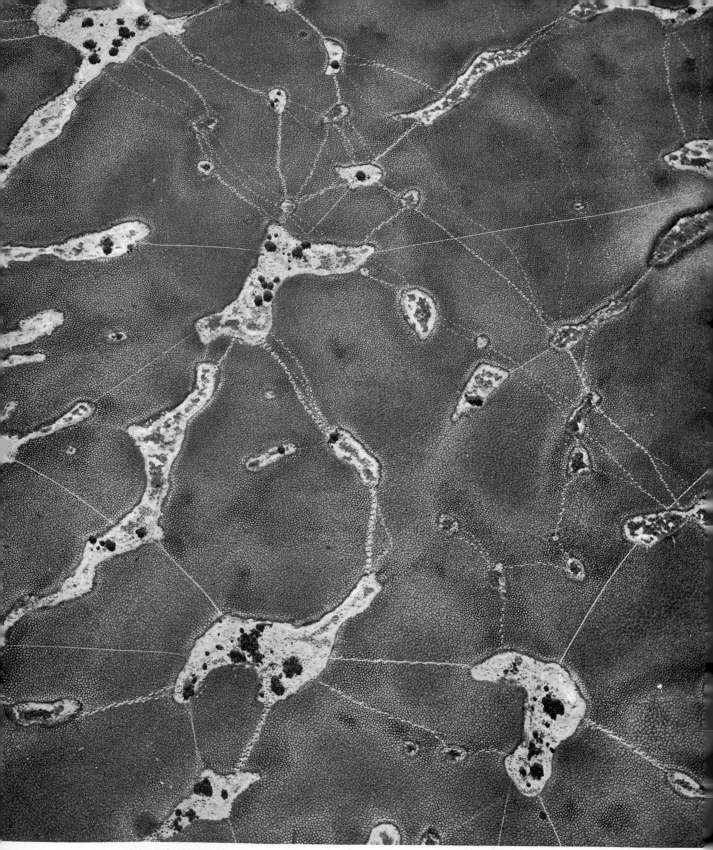

STRAIGHT LINES TO SAFETY are shown in this unusual aerial photograph taken above Soda Lake in California. White patches are high ground with vegetation. The dark areas over most of the picture are hot salt flats. In hurrying from one cool patch to another, rabbits make straight, thin lines and cattle the heavier, dotted lines.

FRESH-WATER SHRIMP SWARM TO LIFE IN A DRY LAKE BED THAT WAS SUDDENLY FILLED BY A DOWNPOUR

Hardy Survivors of Drought

On August 23, 1955, a driving rainstorm exploded over a barren flat in the Mojave Desert. Within a few hours the flat, which had been dust-dry for 25 long years, was covered with 18 inches of muddy water.

Two days later this water was alive with millions of fresh-water shrimp hatched out of eggs buried for those 25 years. A million years ago, when this desert area was a lake, such shrimp hatched regularly every year. But as the climate became drier, the shrimp slowly adjusted by waiting for rain before hatching. Though their life cycle has changed during this long period, the appearance of these shrimp has remained much the same as it was a million years ago.

A ZOOLOGIST digs for shrimp eggs in a dry lake bottom. The eggs remain alive in the hard mud and can survive for perhaps 100 years, waiting for rain before hatching.

RABBITS drink at a water hole in the wilderness of central Australia. Rabbits rarely drink water; they get most of the moisture they need from the vegetation they eat.

But Australia's 500 million rabbits sometimes crop the country's grassland clean and the rabbits are forced to drink. Rabbits were brought to Australia by some English

settlers in 1859. The animals soon spread across large sections of the continent. As they spread, they ate up the pastures and drank the water needed for Australia's sheep. In 1950 scientists tried to kill off the rabbits by infecting them with a virus. Millions died, but others were immune to the disease and survived to spread again.

THE GRAY MASS OF AN APPROACHING CLOUDBURST BEARS DOWN ON SOME OCOTILLO BUSHES IN ITS PATH

Rain: Too Little or Too Much

For months deserts thirst for rain. But when the rains do come, they fall violently. In an hour a cloudburst can spill several inches of water on a valley left dry for 10 years. Rain can drench one side of a trail while leaving the other side without a drop. Falling on scorched ground, rain may evaporate instantly.

Desert storms often cause flash floods because the hard-baked ground cannot absorb rain. The water flows into gulches and channels, then roars downhill, loaded with uprooted plants and torn branches. Finally these torrents reach flat land, and there they form temporary shallow lakes. Much plant and animal life is destroyed by such storms, but the water will supply the means to make life flourish once more.

A STORM OF RAIN AND HAIL MAY LAST ONLY A FEW MINUTES, BUT IT MAY BE THE ONLY WATER FOR A YEAR

A MUD-COLORED FLOOD swirls down a channel worn into the desert floor (*below*). Rain water, unable to sink into the hard ground, rushes off in streams to shallow pools that quickly evaporate. Hours after the storm is over, the channel is empty and dry again. Long roots of a plant that reached for water now lie exposed to the sun.

Tricks of the Desert Air

There is mystery as well as violence in desert life. Clouds may gather above the sands and seem to spill their rain. Yet not a drop may reach the earth. Visions of long lakes may shimmer on the horizon but vanish as the traveler approaches them.

There are reasons for these mysteries. Phantom rain *(right)* begins when cold air high above the desert floor releases a real downpour. But as the rain falls, it enters a lower layer of much hotter air and evaporates there.

The unreal sea *(below)* is a mirage. It is an illusion similar to what takes place when a stick is pushed into a pond. The stick appears to bend where it enters the water. There, the different densities of air and water cause light rays to bend. In the desert, different densities of warm and cool air do just the same. Light rays, coming down through cool air, bend upward as they strike hot air near the ground *(diagram, page 34)*. It is as if a mirror on the desert reflected the blue light of the sky.

RAIN falls from storm clouds above the Sahara. But this rain turns into vapor as it hits the superheated desert air. It evaporates completely, high above the desert palms.

A MIRAGE shines like a sea in the Sahara. This mirage, formed by hot surface air, holds tall islands which are the reflected images of real mountains on the horizon.

111

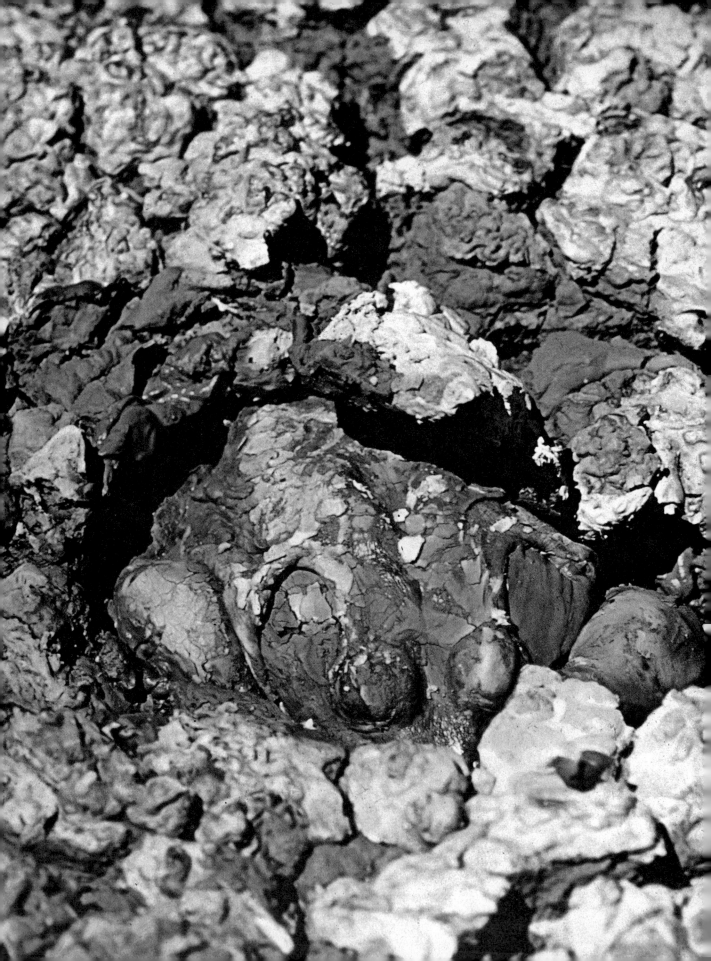

A mud-caked frog *(left)* digs itself
into a mudhole that is drying up.
The frog is trying to escape from
the heat of the desert by burying
itself. But unless there is rain be
fore long, this frog will surely die.

6

Ways of Life
in Dry Lands

All of us are dependent. This is not just the dependence
that children have on their parents. It goes beyond that.

All of us—children and adults alike—are dependent on
hundreds and hundreds of people. They produce the food
we eat, the clothes we wear, the cars we drive, the electricity
that lights our homes and a thousand other things.

Most of them are people we never see and probably never
will see. That is a pity, because if ever we could see all the
people, places and things which influence our lives it would
surely be a sight to remember.

Animals are dependent, too, though of course their needs
are very much simpler than the needs of human beings.

In fact, there is no living thing which is truly independent,
not even the green plants, which make their own food. They
must rely on good weather and proper growing conditions.

Now stop and think a minute. Plants are dependent on
good soil and the proper weather. But are we? Does it
matter to us if plants fail to grow? Indeed it does.

Vegetables come from plants, and so do fruits. The bread
we eat is made mostly of flour, which started out as grain,

the product of a plant. And much of the meat we eat comes from animals that live on plants.

This means that all living things are *interdependent*— that is, the life of one thing often relies very heavily on the well-being of another. But this interdependence is not just between living things. Plants and animals are even further influenced by the sort of place they live in and the kind of climate which is found there.

This is certainly apparent in the deserts. Here drought means hardship, danger and death—while rain brings with it growth and food and life.

Desert Quail

One animal whose well-being is influenced by the amount of rain that falls is the desert quail. In the American Southwest, near Searchlight, Nevada, one kind of desert quail was studied for seven years. It is called the Gambel quail, and the scientist who studied these birds came up with some surprising facts.

He kept track of these quail, and found that in dry years they produced few or no young birds. Most of them never even built nests. But in a wet year, things were entirely different—100 adult quail produced 632 chicks.

Here was a mystery to solve: no chicks one year and large families the next. The scientist first found that in dry years there was little or no green plant food for the quail to eat. Without green food, the adults seemed unable to mate and produce chicks.

But why? That was the question. Studies had shown that vitamin A might be involved. In wet years, when green food was available, the quail had plenty of vitamin A. But in dry years they showed a shortage.

Scientists think that this might be the answer. The lack of vitamin A kept the birds from mating during periods of drought. Where did the vitamin A come from? From green vegetation, which grew mainly in wet years.

So we see how the weather controls the food supply, which in turn may make a difference in the population of animals in the desert. This is an example of interdependence.

Let's take a look now at locusts. Like the quail, locusts have a strange pattern of life, strongly influenced by their surroundings.

Locusts are found in nearly all the dry regions of the world. In some years they become a terrible enemy of crops and pastureland. They group in huge swarms made up of millions and millions of insects. One swarm that was blown over the Red Sea was said to be 2,000 miles long. That is about the distance from New York City to Denver, Colorado. Once, on Cyprus, an island in the Mediterranean Sea, a mass of locust eggs was collected and destroyed. The eggs weighed 2,600,000 pounds. At times, these swarming locusts are so hungry they can chew a field of grain down to the ground in a matter of minutes. They will eat up the fence posts, and even gulp down the laundry on the clotheslines.

However, the really strange thing about locusts is that they have two forms. One is called the *solitary* form, and these locusts prefer to keep to themselves. The solitary locusts are small and pale. They have wings, but these wings are useless, and the solitary locusts cannot fly. Instead they get about by hopping across the ground.

The other form of locust is *gregarious*, which means that they group together into swarms. These gregarious locusts are big and colorful. They have long wings and they are very good fliers. But most important, the gregarious locusts migrate in masses.

For years it was believed that these were two very different insects. Yet a Russian scientist proved that they are actually two different forms of the same insect.

Crowding Changes Locusts

His studies showed it was the conditions they grew up in that decided whether locusts would be the sort that swarmed together or stayed alone.

It was found that most of the time locusts grow up to be the solitary form—those that keep to themselves. These locusts behave like ordinary grasshoppers and do not cause a great deal of damage.

Now, a season of very good weather with plenty of rain

"BREADMAKING" ANTS

Harvester ants store thousands of seeds in their burrows deep under the desert floor. As the seeds are brought in, "chewing societies" husk the seeds and chew them into an edible form, which is called "ant bread." They store this "bread" and it keeps the colony fed during periods when other food is scarce.

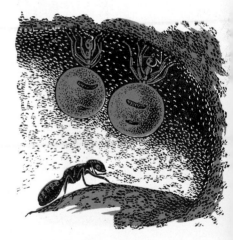

LIVING STOREHOUSES

Honeypot ants of the desert are living storehouses of plant juices. Older worker ants pump the juice into the elastic bodies of young ants. These "honeypots" spend most of their lives hanging from the ceilings of underground nests. They look like tiny Japanese lanterns hanging in a miniature cave.

will result in a large supply of plant food. Such conditions will also cause an increase in the number of solitary locusts, and a certain amount of crowding will result.

It is this crowding which actually leads to the development of the gregarious form of locust. The scientist who did the experiments on locusts showed this in a very simple way. He took a few young locusts and put them in a large cage. Then he took a larger number of young locusts and put them in a small cage. The locusts in the large, uncrowded cage turned into pale solitary locusts. But the locusts crowded into the small cage turned into the large, gregarious form which always bands into swarms.

Now in nature, this sort of crowding may come about when a season of very good weather is followed by a season with a shortage of rain. Food then becomes scarce. The large number of locusts hatched during the good year were already a little crowded. Now they are forced into even more crowded conditions in those areas where food can be found.

These crowded locusts produce a large number of young locusts. Unlike their parents, which were solitary locusts, these young locusts form into bands, which move along, eating as they go. As the band moves, other young locusts join it, and when two groups meet, they unite into one large group. Slowly the swarm of locusts begins to grow.

The Flight of the Locusts

These young locusts have been moving along the ground because their wings have not yet formed. About four weeks after the locusts have hatched, these wings begin to appear, and the locusts make short flights. They feed wherever they land—and it is at this stage that the locusts gobble up almost everything in sight. They are a flying army that destroys as it moves forward. They eat so much that their stomachs are stretched out of shape.

By now, these locusts are the true migratory form—big, spotted and long-winged. Nobody knows exactly why, but now the swarm flies off on one final long flight before the locusts mate and lay eggs.

As they fly off, these millions and millions of locusts have

THE JACK RABBIT

This swift creature can outrun all of its desert enemies. In one leap it can cover 15 feet. But the jack rabbit also is afraid of going too far from its burrow. Thus, when it tries to escape, it runs around in circles. Coyotes and foxes are aware of this. They catch the jack rabbit by patiently lying in ambush.

no idea where they are headed. In some cases they just go in whatever direction the wind takes them—and whole swarms may fly off to sea and drown.

They fly for as long as three days and nights, and sometimes travel hundreds of miles. Then, wherever they happen to land, they eat once more if there is anything to eat. After that, the eggs are laid and the adult locusts die.

One generation of locusts is gone. What will the next one be? Will they be swarmers—or the smaller solitary locusts? That will depend first on how many eggs are laid in one place. It will also depend on the sort of conditions found when the new locusts hatch. Is there vegetation nearby? And if not, will rain fall in the springtime, bringing the green plants up to provide food? The locusts' pattern of life will be decided by these conditions.

Harvester Ants

Let's look now at a desert creature which gets along in quite a different way from the locust or the desert quail. This is the harvester ant. These ants live in deep underground nests, and they have developed a way of life which allows them to get along in heat or cold, rain or drought. They have a regular daily routine and there is little change in the number of ants in each ant colony from year to year. Scientists call this a "stable" way of life, meaning that it shows very few ups and downs.

But deserts are places which have long periods of drought and occasional violent rains. As we have seen, these conditions affect the lives of many desert animals. Most desert insects appear only after wet weather has brought forth plant life. But harvester ants are alert and busy all year long. How do these insects manage to have such a stable way of life?

To find the answer, one interested scientist went to the California desert to study the life of harvester ants. He found that these ants had organized their lives to solve the two most difficult problems of getting along in the desert: avoiding the heat and having enough food to exist during the long dry spells when plants are scarce.

To avoid the killing heat, harvester ants do two things.

They live in burrows 15 or more feet underground, and they only leave the burrow at times when the ground above is cool. Worker teams of ants go out early in the morning when the temperature is low (40° to 50°). For two or three hours they go about their task of gathering seeds for food and bringing them back to the nest. Before the ground gets really hot, the ants return to their tunnels.

How "Ant Bread" Is Made

The ants stay underground all day and only come up again to forage in the cool of the evening. The food-gathering trips of these ants keep the colony fed from day to day. But they also provide a store of seeds for periods when food is scarce. During the dry season, the everyday diet of the harvester ants is made up of the seeds of two common plants called the woolly plantain and the comb-bur.

Every day a supply of these seeds is brought back to the burrow. Here there is a special group of ants organized into what are called "chewing societies." It is their job to remove the husks from the seeds and chew them into a kind of crumbly mass called ant bread, which the ants eat.

Each day they eat as much as they need. Whatever is left over is stored for future use. There are many tunnels in the ants' large underground nests, and on the lower levels there are special storage chambers for food.

This stored food will be eaten only during the hottest summer days, when the heat makes work outside danger-ous, and during the cold rainy season.

Once a year harvester ants enjoy a change from their everyday diet. This is after the rains have brought a new growth of plants with a fresh crop of seeds. Then the workers suddenly stop gathering their everyday diet of plantain and comb-bur seeds and switch to the seeds of other plants. When the hot, dry season begins again, the ant colony goes back to its regular food.

It takes hard work to have this sort of life in the desert. The scientist who studied the harvester ants in the California desert counted the seeds gathered by a single colony in a single day. There were 7,000 of them. Within a space of

THE CHAIN OF LIFE

The chain of survival in the desert begins with plants *(bottom)*. These make their own food from sunlight, air and water. These plants are the food of such small animals as the cricket, and the cricket in its turn serves as prey for larger animals such as the desert spiny lizard. A lizard may provide dinner for a snake, and the snake may be hunted down by a ravenous road runner. Finally, the road runner may be devoured by a large flesh eater like the ring-tail cat, shown at the top. Thus each life depends on another.

one acre of ground the scientist found that there were six harvester-ant colonies. So on that one acre, the ants probably harvested 42,000 seeds a day.

By studying ants, locusts and quail, we have seen how the desert influences the lives of these creatures. Now let us turn things around and see how animals may make changes in their surroundings.

Let us see, for example, what happens if men put cattle out to graze on dry pastureland. These cattle eat up all the natural grasses and edible shrubs, thereby making a place for weeds and cactuses to grow, and shrubs like the mesquite, which the cattle cannot eat.

Such a change in vegetation will also change the kind of animals that can live on the land. Once the cattle have eaten up the grass, their pasture is destroyed and they must leave. Many of the other creatures which live in the grassy places must also leave. In time these creatures are replaced by those animals that can live in areas of desert vegetation.

The jack rabbit is one such animal. Jack rabbits actually increase in number where the land has been "skinned" by grazing. This is because their main food in the dry season is mesquite. As we have learned, the mesquite springs up when the natural grass has been destroyed by overgrazing.

The Rabbit in Australia

A striking example of the way a region can be changed from grassland to desert is found in Australia. In 1859, two dozen rabbits were brought from Europe and turned loose on a ranch in southern Australia. Soon their number began to increase. Within three years, the ranch was overrun with them. The rabbits began to spread out, moving north and west at the rate of about 70 miles a year. By 1900 the whole southern portion of Australia had millions and millions of rabbits. This increase in rabbits occurred after Australia's sheepherding industry had started to expand—and the rabbits invaded the pasturelands. The sheep cropped the green plants down to the ground, and the rabbits ate whatever was left. Together with the sheep, the rabbits turned much of the Australian pastureland into wasteland. Today dust storms and drifting sand blow across what once was green grazing land. And so, with the thoughtless help of man, animals have changed and ruined the land they lived on.

The rabbits in Australia became so destructive it was decided that they had to be destroyed. In 1950 the virus of a disease called myxomatosis (mix-o-mah-*toe*-sis), or rabbit pox, was used to infect a number of rabbits. This disease makes rabbits swell up and die. The virus spread very quickly and rabbits died by the millions.

Today the rabbit is scarce in Australia. Plants grow again in places where they had little chance to grow before. Slowly the land is recovering from the damage done to it. Sheep are still an important part of Australia's business, but now the sheepherders of Australia know they must be careful. If their sheep are allowed to overgraze the land, the desert conditions may come back.

Flesh Eaters and Plant Eaters

So far we have seen how animals can change the land they live on. We have also seen how the climate and plant life of the desert may influence the animals. Now another question comes up. How do animals influence each other? What is the relationship between the plant eaters and the meat eaters?

Here we come back to a word we learned at the beginning of this chapter. It is *interdependence*. This interdependence begins with plants. If there is plenty of rain, the plants will have a good season for growing. Many seeds will be produced. In fact, the plants will produce so many seeds that there will be plenty for a new crop of plants the next rainy season— even though most of the seed crop is eaten by animals.

So we see that most of the seed crop for one year never grows into new plants. It is eaten by animals. The same is true of the animals themselves. The mice which ate the seeds will raise families, of which only a few will escape being eaten by larger, flesh-eating animals. Thus, the welfare of the larger animals depends upon the smaller creatures.

And so, all living things are interdependent, and their general welfare can be traced back to such basic things as the weather and the land.

A PACK RAT CAUTIOUSLY AVOIDS A CLUSTER OF SPINES TO NIBBLE ON A SECTION OF PRICKLY PEAR CACTUS

Plant Protection

Green plants provide food and moisture for many of the animals which live in the desert. But many desert plants have tough stems and sharp spines, which give them some protection against hungry animals. Others have bitter or poisonous juices. But no form of defense gives plants complete protection.

121

A BRONZED CHENOPOD, an Arabian Desert shrub, grows in scattered clumps. These plants are widely spaced since each uses all available water in its vicinity. For this reason, no other plants will grow nearby. Sand piles up around each plant, and the older the plant the higher its little dune. Chenopods have poisonous juices.

Thorns: Danger and Haven

As a protection for plants, thorns are most effective against large animals. But many small birds and rodents find safety in these thorny plants. The tree-shaped cholla often has tenants. A cactus wren is much safer nesting among the cholla's barbs than it would be in a less prickly dwelling. Ground squirrels and pack rats climb up the cholla's stems to feed on its juicy fruits. But to bigger animals the forbidding cholla bristles with unpleasantness. Its barbs catch on anything that touches them. Actually this is one way the plant reproduces itself. Small pieces, carried away on clothing or fur, take root when dropped on the ground. Pieces of the plant also drop to the ground and grow where they fall, as seen opposite.

← **JUMPING CHOLLA,** pronounced "choy-yuh" *(left),* is so named because its stems break off at the slightest touch and seem to leap out to fasten onto animal skin or fur.

BOOJUM TREE stores water in its cone-shaped trunk *(right).* After a rain, leaves sprout all over it. When they fall, their stems remain on the plant and form thorns.

GRAZING SHEEP of a North African Berber tribe strip an arid area of its vegetation. The sheep nibble plants down to the ground. Their sharp hoofs also injure many shallow, tender plant roots. This kind of overgrazing will finally turn such a poor region into an actual desert.

A CLOUD OF LOCUSTS swarms above a field *(opposite)* ▶ in Kenya, Africa. Locusts are common in dry lands and destroy huge areas of vegetation. They can eat up a field of grain in a few minutes. Locusts have been known even to eat fence posts and clothes drying on a clothesline.

7

Peoples of the Desert

We all know that people live in deserts. We have seen pictures of nomads, or wandering tribesmen, wearing long robes and riding across the sand dunes. We know about camel caravans that plod across the desert. And an oasis brings to mind the picture of women carrying jars of water from a well.

Thus the idea of people living in deserts is not very surprising. But if we stop to think, we wonder why they do. Why in the world would anybody choose to live in the desert? Yet people have done so for hundreds and even thousands of years.

People have clustered around an oasis and planted date-palm trees. They have farmed tiny patches of land and traded their produce with passing caravans. They have herded small bands of goats onto the almost barren hillsides and watched over the animals as they grazed. They have milked the goats and made cheese. And they have made clothes and tents from goatskin.

Some tribes have become wealthy traders in the deserts. Others have become wealthy pirates—swooping down to rob

127

caravans loaded with rare spices, rich cloth and ivory.

The most complete record of people living in the desert is probably found in the Sahara. You will see that it is an amazing story.

One of the first people to look into the history of the Sahara and its tribes was a German professor by the name of Henry Barth. He set out from Germany as a young man in 1849, and spent six long years traveling and exploring the desert of northern Africa.

Most of the tribesmen Barth met had never even seen a European person before. And they were astonished by what he did. Twice Barth crossed the great Sahara, and one tribe was so amazed that he had come through alive that they gave him a nickname: "The man who goes through fire."

Barth returned home in 1855. He took with him maps he had drawn of the regions he had explored. But even more important, Barth brought back with him some startling news about the history of the Sahara.

In the northern Sahara, Barth had found pictures carved and painted on the sides of cliffs. These pictures showed scenes of life in the Sahara in ancient times. But the amazing thing is that they were not scenes of desert life. They were pictures of horses and bulls and antelopes, which are not animals of the desert. And some of these pictures showed people watching over herds of grazing cattle.

What Barth had discovered was that the Sahara, at some time long ago, had not been the dry, empty land it later became. Instead, it was a fertile land, actually swampy in parts. And it was filled with life of all kinds—including plants, animals and people.

Desert Pictures Tell a Story

Since Barth's first discoveries, more than 30,000 different pictures have been found in the Sahara. All together, these pictures are like a storybook. They are an amazing record of a lost world, painted by many generations of tribesmen over a period of almost 8,000 years. They show the area as it was seen by different artists at different times. Thus, as the area changed, these paintings recorded the change. That is, they show the gradual change of a green, wet land, rich with forests, into a barren wasteland of endless sand and stone.

A great many of these pictures were discovered on a high tableland with the difficult name of Tassili-n-Ajjer, which means "the plateau of the rivers." This plateau is in the mountains of southern Algeria.

In general, these pictures show what life was like during four different stages in the region. The earliest of these stages is shown in pictures made about 10,000 years ago. The pictures tell us that the plateau, and the land around it, was an area with many rivers. Lions roamed the hills, and large herds of animals lived on the grassy plains. Some of these animals, such as the oxen and buffalo, were tame. Other animals shown in these pictures were wild and included elephants, giraffes and rhinoceroses.

The people who painted these pictures were hunters. We know this because they are shown going after game armed with hand axes and boomerangs.

Paintings of Desert Herdsmen

The second stage in this story of the Sahara is seen in paintings made about 4,000 years later. From these paintings we can see that there was still plenty of water in the region. One picture shows men in reed boats hunting hippopotamuses.

In fact, hunting was still an important part of the people's lives—though with some changes. The pictures show that the hunters rarely used axes and boomerangs. Their weapons were now bows and arrows.

This second stage of the picture story also tells us that the area was still rich and green, because huge herds of cattle are shown grazing. This is an important fact, because it shows that these people had learned how to raise their own animals for meat. One picture, 40 feet long, shows men driving a band of 65 cattle.

It is in the pictures showing the third stage that we become aware that something was happening to the land. The climate of the region was becoming drier because it was getting much less rain, and rivers were drying up.

The pictures of this stage were carved and painted a little

DESERT TRIBES

Desert dwellers in Africa occupy two large areas, in the north and in the south. This map shows the names of the tribes who live in the north. The desert to the south is the Kalahari-Namib, and here the Bushmen live. The Bushman tribes have never been counted. They lead a hunter's life, move constantly and carry their water supply with them in empty ostrich eggs.

more than 3,500 years ago. Now, for the first time, there are pictures of horses. These horses were brought in by travelers from eastern Africa. They are shown pulling wooden plows and chariots.

This tells us much about the people living during this period. The chariots tell us that these desert people probably traveled away from home and visited other people, from whom they may have learned new skills. Chariots are also used in war, so we may guess that these people fought with their neighbors from time to time.

The scenes with horses pulling plows are very important, too. By now these people had learned how to farm, and no longer had to depend on hunting.

But again, the pictures show that the land was changing. There are only a few paintings of animals which need a lot of water. Cattle and elephants are rarely shown—and there are no pictures at all of the rhinoceros, hippopotamus and many other wild animals.

The Land Dries Up

So now we come to the fourth stage, as shown in the cliff pictures. These date back to about 2,500 years ago. The changes are amazing.

The land was not yet quite a desert, but it was very dry—and getting drier. We know this because there is not a single picture of a large wild animal. There was hardly enough water even for the horses, and paintings of horses became fewer and fewer. In place of the horse, the camel came into use, because only the camel could survive the dry conditions as the land began to wither.

Soon after that, the paintings show a real change. Many of the early pictures were very carefully made and quite beautiful. But near the end, the paintings become crude and carelessly done. This probably means that the last of the cliff painters to live on this once fertile plateau had moved away or died out. Those who came after them probably lived a much simpler life.

These crude pictures are the last record of human life on the plateau. After that, the record comes to an end.

What was it that changed half of Africa from a land of green forests and large herds of animals into a bleak desert? No one will ever know for sure, of course. But most scientists believe it was the work of natural forces which brought about a change of climate. The area came under the influence of blistering dry winds—the kinds of winds we learned about in Chapter 2.

The Camel

As we have seen, the camel was brought to the desert after water had become so scarce that there was no longer enough for horses. Without this curious beast, which can get along for days without water and food, much of the travel in the Sahara would have been impossible.

And so the camel has been a blessing. But in some ways, the camel is a curse as well. One Arab story says that when God made camels He forgot to give them a brain. Instead He gave them extra stomachs. Another Arab proverb says there are 11,000 devils in the head of one camel.

And the truth is that camels are both stupid and moody. Many people think that camels are born knowing all about how to get along in the desert. The fact is they don't even know how to walk on sand. They have to be taught. And if a camel goes awhile without walking on sand, it may have to be taught all over again.

There is an old legend that says camels never lose their way in the desert. The legend says that if a desert traveler gets lost, all he has to do is let loose the reins of his camel and "the ship of the desert," as camels are called, will find its way home.

Nothing could be further from the truth. Arab camel drivers will tell you that a single camel, feeding with a herd, sometimes gets so interested in the joy of eating a special plant that it will not notice that the rest of the herd has wandered away. It may not even notice the approach of darkness. But suddenly it looks up to see that night has come. Then, not only will the camel be unable to find its way home, but it will become quite terrified of being lost, and it will begin to run around in circles and moan.

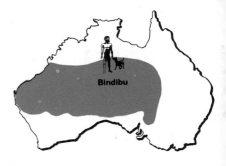

BINDIBU TRIBES

The Bindibu tribesmen are known to inhabit parts of the west central desert of Australia, though their number is unknown. Small bands wander widely in unexplored areas in search of food. An expedition team searching for Bindibu found a band—but there were only 40 in it.

That is yet another annoying thing about camels—they love to moan. They moan when they are loaded, and they moan when they are unloaded. And often they moan for no reason at all—just because they feel like moaning.

Sometimes male camels grow mean. They will bite each other and they will bite people, too. If they are too far away to bite a man, they may just spit some smelly stomach juice into his face. The camels are so temperamental that sometimes, if they do not like the food they are given, they will starve themselves to death just for spite. But when camels are in a gentle mood, a young child can lead a string of six or seven animals without any trouble.

Although the camel seems to be as hard to live with as the desert itself, it is made to serve in many ways. It is not only an important means of desert travel, but also a source of food and drink. Camel meat is often eaten, although it is dry and tough and tastes like a leathery steak. Camel milk is a common desert drink. The cheese made from the milk is a usual part of a nomad's diet. Camel wool is useful too. It is spun and woven into clothes and strong tent cloth. Leather made from the camel's hide is used in making pouches and sandals.

The Bushmen

Though hundreds and hundreds of years have gone by since the camel first came to the desert, the life of the desert people has changed very little. In fact, their clothing and their customs have not changed much in the past 2,000 years. This is especially true of the Bushmen.

The Bushmen are a people found south of the Sahara, in Africa's Kalahari Desert. They lead an uncertain life. It is so uncertain that it is hard for us to imagine it. The Bushmen live from one day to the next, never knowing if they are going to get enough to eat—or anything to eat at all.

All they have to rely on is their wonderful knowledge of nature. But for them, this is quite enough. As a result, even though they have so little, the Bushmen are a self-reliant and very happy people.

Not long ago a scientist visited a tribe of Bushmen and

watched a Bushman artist at work. The Bushman sang and laughed. To him, the animals he was drawing were his friends, and he had stories to tell about each one of them.

Bushmen believe that men, animals, insects and all life are made out of the same stuff—and that they all belong to the same family. Although the Bushmen must hunt to live, they have deep respect for the animals they kill. Often they sing songs of praise and gratitude before they cut up an antelope and cook it to eat.

It is difficult to describe how close these people are to nature. But they seem to have an instinct for the world they live in—what we might call a "sixth sense."

Desert Hunters

For example, one old tribesman told the visiting scientist that he knew when he was going to have a lucky day hunting. On such a morning, the Bushman said, he knew he would kill an animal, because he could already "feel" the blood of the animal dripping on his heels as he carried it home. This old tribesman also said he could "feel" the approach of a faraway herd of animals because he could "feel" the stripes of the animals on his skin.

But Bushmen cannot rely on animals for food. In fact a dinner of meat is fairly rare with them. Instead, these people often must be content with a meal made of plants, roots, berries and seeds—and with luck, a lizard or two.

The Bushmen know all there is to know about the plants found in their homeland. They know where each kind grows, and when its seeds or berries will be ripe for eating. And every plant has a use. Most are for food, of course, but others are used for medicine, and some are used for making the color dyes with which they paint pictures. One special plant is useful to make the poison in which the Bushmen dip their arrows before they go out to hunt. This poison slows down the wounded animals so the hunters can track them.

Like all desert dwellers, Bushmen have the problem of getting enough water. They have solved the problem as well as it can be solved by a simple, wandering people living in a desert wasteland.

PAINTINGS OF ANCIENT DESERT PEOPLE

RUNNING MAN

A rock painting of a running man, dated about 8000 B.C., is the oldest of many paintings found in a cave on the high Tassili-n-Ajjer Plateau region of central Sahara.

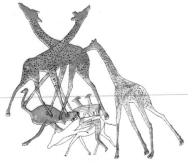

WILDLIFE

The giraffe, ostrich and antelope in this rock painting indicate that the Sahara once was covered with enough green vegetation to support herds of grass-eating animals.

COW AND ARCHER

The artist who painted this cow and archer 6,000 years ago moved with a tribe that herded animals in the Saharan plateau. But today this area is a barren wasteland.

Each band of Bushmen has its own water holes. Often these are so small and hidden that a stranger would never even notice them. But the Bushman knows exactly where he can dig down and suck up the water he needs.

So we see that the Bushmen are really a sensitive people. They are aware of everything around them. They have a deep respect for nature—and they find delight and beauty in it, too. This love of nature is shown in their paintings. These paintings are much like the early pictures found on the cliff sides at Tassili-n-Ajjer, which also showed a real love of nature.

The Kalahari Desert, where the Bushmen live, is so barren that almost no outsiders ever go there, and so the Bushmen are left alone. They get along chiefly by hunting, and therefore they are a wandering people, who move about as they need to in order to find food. But some desert dwellers are a settled people who have lived in the same places for hundreds of years. Among these are the Mozabites.

The Mozabites

There are about 40,000 Mozabite people. They live in one of the hottest, rockiest and most desolate regions of the Sahara, miles and miles from any neighboring towns.

But here, in this unfriendly place, the Mozabites have built large cities. All together, there are five cities, and the largest has 16,000 people living in it.

The Mozabites have been able to live in the same place for a long time because they are a very hard-working group of people. Many centuries ago they dug 3,000 wells down through more than a hundred feet of solid limestone. With the water from these wells, they are able to irrigate more than 200,000 date-palm trees. They can also grow oranges, apricots, figs and olives. The Mozabites have also grown rich as traders.

The Mozabites lead a kind of double life. When they deal with outsiders, they speak the Arabic language and conduct themselves just like everyone else. But among themselves they are quite different.

They speak their own very different language, and every-

VARIOUS SHELTERS FOR DESERT LIVING

INDIAN PUEBLO

This Indian pueblo looks much like an apartment house built of dried mud. As the population grows, rooms are added. Ladders serve as stairs. The largest known pueblo in New Mexico once had 800 rooms.

NAVAJO HOGAN

A Navajo hogan is a frame of logs covered with thick layers of mud. These thick mud walls keep this practical dwelling fairly cool during the heat of the summer days and warm at night and in the winter.

thing they do is in accordance with their religion, which is very strict. The laws of the tribe are made by the religious leaders. One such law is that a Mozabite, regardless of how rich he may be, is required to live in a very simple way, and must never make any display of personal wealth. In fact it is considered very bad manners to be seen wearing anything but the plainest clothes.

But these strict rules also serve a good purpose. Living according to these rules, the Mozabites have been able to prosper for nearly a thousand years in one of the unfriendliest regions of the world.

The Tuareg

There is in the Sahara another kind of desert people. They do not hunt as the Bushmen do and most of them do not live in communities as the Mozabites do. These are the colorful Tuareg (*Twah*-reg) tribes. They are an ancient people of the desert who are found scattered over a large area of the Sahara.

The Tuareg are generally tall people, with large noses and straight, dark hair. Both men and women wear long, billowing pantaloons, which are almost always dark blue or black. Over these they wear a loose white cotton shirt, which looks something like an old-fashioned nightshirt. On the outside, the Tuareg wear a huge robe, which is sometimes white, sometimes striped with lavender and sometimes dark blue-black. The women never cover their faces, but the men and boys always veil their faces so completely that only their eyes can be seen. For this reason they are called "the veiled men of the Sahara."

Long ago, the Tuareg were dreaded by other people in the Sahara. They raised a special sort of camel with very long legs which could outrun all other camels. Mounted on these swift "riding camels," the Tuareg charged down on desert caravans and robbed them of their goods. In time, the fierce Tuareg became so dreaded that merchants had to bribe them to leave their caravans alone.

In addition to robbing caravans, the Tuareg were engaged in slave trading. Tuareg bands traveled south of the Sahara and took captives whom they later sold, mostly to Europeans.

TUAREG ZERIBA

A Tuareg *zeriba* is built of grass which is laid over a wooden frame. It may be 15 feet square and 10 feet high. Tuareg people use this kind of dwelling to provide shelter during the hot spells in the desert.

BEDOUIN TENT

A Bedouin tent, made of goat-hair cloth, is stretched over lightweight poles. This open shelter always is pitched with its opening away from the wind. The floor often is covered with lovely handmade wool rugs.

MONGOL YURT

This Mongol yurt is a light tent used by wandering tribes of Central Asia. The yurt is made of springy willow poles covered with felt or fur and is easy to take down and pack up when the tribe moves on.

135

However, in the 1800s, when European nations took control of large parts of Africa, soldiers were sent to tame the wild ways of the Tuareg.

Today different tribes of Tuareg live in several different ways. Their big "riding camels" are still famous, and some Tuareg raise these swift animals for sale. Others specialize in raising herds of goats, cattle and sheep. A few Tuareg tribes have turned to farming and raise grain and dates, which they trade with other people of the Sahara for products they need.

But the sad thing is that some desert experts believe that the Tuareg may be a disappearing group of people. Outsiders have forced them to change their way of life, and they have not adjusted very well. Many of them are farmers, but the regions where they live have very poor soil. The Tuareg who raise herds of animals have the same problem: they lack good pastureland.

It is true, these tribes used to live by robbing others—but they are a daring people with a proud history. Should the Tuareg die out, the Sahara would lose its most colorful group of people.

The Choice of a Desert Home

Now we come back to the question asked at the beginning of this chapter. Why in the world would anybody choose to live in the desert?

There is no single answer. The Mozabites chose to live in the desert to escape enemies who objected to their strict religious views.

In the case of the Bushmen, they were actually driven into the desert by white settlers who took over their homeland about 300 years ago. But as we have seen, the Bushmen have certainly adjusted well to desert life.

Finally, we find such people as the Tuareg, who wander over parts of the Sahara. Nobody knows why the Tuareg are desert dwellers. So far as anyone knows, the Tuareg have lived in the Sahara since the beginning of mankind. In fact, there are some experts who believe that the Tuareg may be the descendants of the skilled people who first painted the many beautiful pictures on the sides of the cliffs in the Sahara.

ROBED AS A PROTECTION AGAINST THE SUN, TUAREG TRIBESMEN OF THE SAHARA LOOK ALMOST LIKE GHOSTS

The Life of Desert Folk

All through history men have lived in the desert, striving with more or less success against the difficulties they face there. Although the Egyptians were able to create a civilization of great magnificence, other desert peoples such as the Tuareg and the Bushmen have had to struggle just to survive.

137

The Tuareg

The Tuareg of the Sahara are an ancient people with a colorful past. For centuries they survived by robbing caravans and by accepting bribes not to molest desert travelers. Colonists from Europe put a stop to the raids. Now these nomads herd camels, goats, sheep and cattle. There are three classes of Tuareg. The nobles are the warriors and leaders. The subjects tend to the flocks. The servants care for the crops and do housework. The Tuareg wear billowing clothes that let cool air swirl about inside.

A SLAVE BOY peers out from his heavy robe *(left)*. He is a descendant of ancient Tuareg captives. Though still a slave, he is well cared for and happy doing housework

A TUAREG TRIBESMAN digs → up an allium *(right)*, a food resembling asparagus but related to the onion. The allium is a hardy plant, easy to grow and very nourishing.

SIMPLE HUTS called *zeribas* *(below)* are made from dry grass. These are hot-weather huts. In winter, the Tuareg use skin tents and pile grass around the sides for warmth.

The Parched World of the Arab

The Tuareg make up only a small part of what is called the Arab World. That world extends from the Atlantic Ocean to the Persian Gulf, and contains nearly 100 million people. They differ in their languages and in the way some cling to old customs while others are very modern. Yet Arabs have some things in common. Camels are still their chief form of travel and dates are their main crop. Most Arabs are Moslems.

A GRUNTING CAMEL is forced down for loading Camels can be very stubborn. Unless given the food it wants, a camel may starve itself to death, just to be spiteful.

A DANCING DRUMMER leads an Arab welcome for a ➤ truck convoy *(right)*. This unit arrived in 1950. It was the first of its kind to cross the Sahara from east to west.

ARAB WOMEN sit cross-legged on a mat-covered street and prepare to worship. In keeping with custom, they have removed their shoes. One pair is shown at the bottom of the picture. The religion of these women is Islam, and its god is called Allah. During the past month these women have eaten very little in preparation for a reli-

gious holiday. They have now gathered to pray and thank Allah for his goodness. The followers of the Islamic faith are called Moslems. Their religion was founded by the prophet Mohammed around A.D. 600, after a vision appeared to him in the city of Mecca in Saudi Arabia. Moslems pray five times a day, facing in the direction of Mecca.

A DOUBLE-DECKER BRIDGE has pointed arches and is decorated with colored stones. This old bridge is in the city of Isfahan, Iran, deep in the desert. It crosses a river called Zayan-deh Rud. Because of the river, this city is a major source of water along the routes used by caravans.

TALL PALMS AND HIGH WALLS border a sandy street in → Faya-Largeau *(right)*, in the African Republic of Chad. Deep wells water the nearby grain fields and date-palm groves of this oasis city, which has 50,000 inhabitants. It is an important stop on the north-south caravan route.

The Great Valley of the Nile

Egypt covers a large section of the Sahara, and most of the country is a sandy wasteland. But flowing the length of this parched land is the Nile River, a majestic ribbon of water 1,600 miles long. The river is so big, and it carries such a great volume of water, that its flow has never once stopped —even though it passes through a longer

THIS STONE STATUE is a 3,200-year-old likeness of a King of Egypt. Partially submerged when the Nile overflows every spring, it will soon be moved to a museum.

THE ABU SIMBEL TEMPLE is guarded by giant statues ➤ carved in stone *(right)*. It is being cut out and lifted up so that the waters of the new Nile dam will not flood it.

stretch of empty dryness than any other river in the world. Because of the Nile, most of Egypt's population has always been crowded close to the river. Only here is there life-giving water to permit farming. The area was the location of one of history's greatest civilizations. The ancient Egyptians were the people who produced the Sphinx, the Great Pyramids and the statues shown on these pages.

The rainy season in the heart of Africa, where the Nile begins, makes the river overflow each spring. Crops planted then produce large harvests, but there are still too many mouths to feed. A huge dam is being built to irrigate additional acres.

RUINS OF THE VALLEY OF TOMBS still stand in the desert near the ancient city of Palmyra in Syria, a country south of Turkey. The crumbled stone towers mark the locations of burial plots, each set aside for a separate family. Much of Palmyra is now a deserted ruin. But at the time of Christ, it was a flourishing city, engaged in

the rich caravan trade. Palmyra's importance was based on the fact that it was the only place with a reliable water source in the midst of the Syrian desert. Later, the trade route which took caravans to Palmyra was changed to a more convenient one to the south. After that, Palmyra ceased to be important and later the city was abandoned.

149

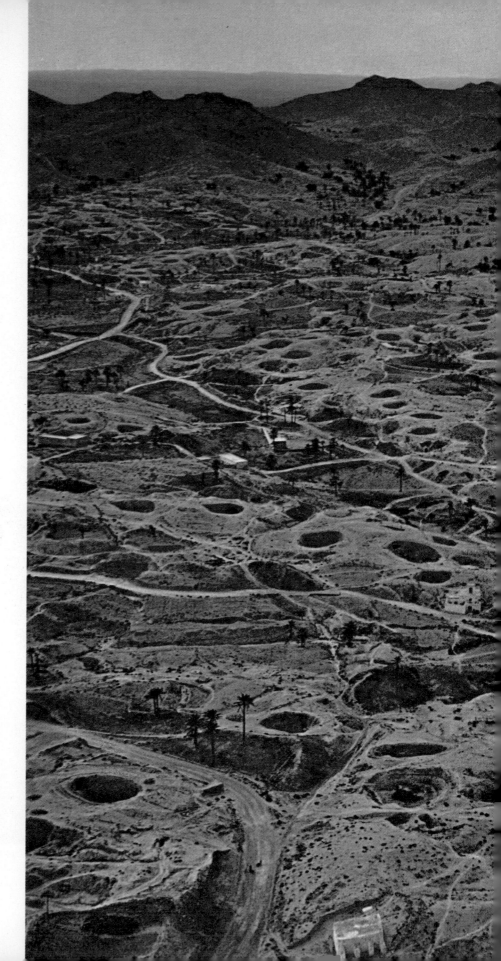

CRATERLIKE PITS make this area of Tunisia look almost like a moon landscape. The strange holes are entrances to underground corridors and rooms occupied by cave dwellers, whose ancestors have lived in this area for 2,000 years. Their underground homes protect them from both desert heat and cold. The Tunisian Government has tried to move them to ordinary homes, but the people prefer to remain here.

150

A BAND OF WEARY BUSHMEN rest as they wait for the day's kill, an ostrich, to be cooked. Game is scarce in the Bushmen's hunting ground, the Kalahari Desert. Such a meal as this is rare. Usually Bushmen live on nuts and roots. Nights are cold, with temperatures as low as 20°. Then Bushmen huddle close together around the fire.

The Bushmen

When Dutch pioneers first explored South Africa in 1652, they found an odd breed of men. The Dutch named them "Bushmen" after the bushy coastal region in which these small people were discovered.

More than 300 years have passed since the Dutch arrived. During that time, the number of Bushmen has dropped from several million to only a few thousand as a result of prolonged fighting between the Bushmen and their enemies.

At the same time, the Bushmen have been driven into the barren Kalahari Desert. Today they are among the most self-reliant people on earth. They wear almost no clothing, have no dwellings, plant no crops and have almost no tools or weapons. And yet they are able to survive and seem to enjoy their demanding way of life.

AN EMPTY OSTRICH SHELL serves as a cup for this little girl. Bushmen store water in the shells and bury them deep in the sand to use during periods of drought.

A PROUD YOUNG HUNTER searches the countryside for game. In his hand he holds a throwing stick, used for killing game. Over his shoulder hangs a tobacco pouch.

153

LEARNING TO HUNT, a young boy is taught by an elder of the band to use the bow and arrow. The arrows are not feathered and are accurate only at short distances.

THREE HUNTERS return to camp with fresh meat. By custom the part of the animal around the spear wound is eaten by the hunters. The rest is taken back to the tribe.

◄ **SPEAR RAISED,** a hunter *(left)* closes in on an antelope. Bushmen who wound a large animal must often track it for days until it dies. Their spears have poisoned tips.

GLEEFULLY LEAPING over a sand dune, a boy takes his turn in a follow-the-leader game. Bushman parents are kind to their children and allow them a great deal of freedom. But young people take on adult duties early. Boys join fathers in the hunt at seven. At the same age, girls join their mothers in hunting for fruits and nuts.

DROP BY DROP, with great patience, a man sucks water out of a damp hole in the sand. His hollow reed is fitted with a grass filter so that he will not get sand in his mouth.

THREE PEOPLE build a simple shelter. It will serve as a windbreak and hold heat from the campfire. Such shelters are the only kind that the roving Bushmen build.

THE WRINKLED FACE of an old Bushman contrasts with ➤ the smooth skin of a baby. Dry, hot winds cause early wrinkles, making Bushmen look older than they are.

The Bindibu

The Bindibu are a small tribe of black men who roam the rocky wasteland of Australia's central-western desert. They are a primitive tribe. They live the way men did thousands of years ago. They have no herds, no crops, no homes, no clothes, no pots for storing food or water, no arts and very few tools.

What they do have is a great will to live. It is this will, and a marvelous understanding of the wilderness they live in, which has kept the Bindibu alive for some 10,000 years in the Australian desert.

The secret of the Bindibu's survival is that they never struggle against nature. Instead, they have learned to obey and use it. They are a wandering people who know the climate of their region so well that they can follow the changing rain patterns across their arid countryside. And the animals they hunt also follow these moving rain patterns.

The Bindibu are grouped into small bands which can move quickly—and which can survive on the small food supplies they find. The men go out each day to hunt birds and wallabies, a kind of kangaroo. The women and children search for grass, roots, seeds, lizards and beetle grubs.

The Bindibu live in such a remote area, and they move about so much, that no one knew they even existed until recently.

A HUNTER AND HIS DOG rest in the water. These dogs are trained to track as pups. After two or three years, the dogs go wild and then are hunted themselves as game.

MOTHERS play with their children after collecting a bit of food. Bindibu men may take more than one wife as a practical way of adding food gatherers to their families.

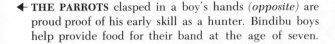

← **THE PARROTS** clasped in a boy's hands (*opposite*) are proud proof of his early skill as a hunter. Bindibu boys help provide food for their band at the age of seven.

159

A Few Skills for a Simple Life

The needs of the Bindibu are simple and so their skills are few. They have grown used to the desert's extremes of heat and cold and therefore they have not learned to make clothes or any lasting shelters. But the few tools that they do need, they make well. The men have excellent stone axes, tied with thongs made of the sinews of a kangaroo. They also carve a boomeranglike throwing stick to bring down birds. They boil a sticky glue from grass and use it to bind stone tips to their spears. Women braid rope (below) and from wood of a native tree make tools for digging roots.

A **BIG TUFT** of dry grass (*above*) is carried into camp on a man's head. The Bindibu use these tufts to shield them from the wind as they sleep by their fires at night.

USING THEIR TOES, THESE BINDIBU WOMEN BRAID FIBERS INTO ROPE. THE ROPE WILL BE USED FOR SLINGS

A CHOCOLATE-BROWN BABY, plump and healthy 'in spite of its constant exposure to the weather, munches happily on its only toy, a stringy piece of bark. Bindibu children are given no playthings, but their parents treat them affectionately and never scold for misbehavior. Bindibu people vary in color from brown to almost black.

BINDIBU TRIBESMEN get down on their hands and knees to drink from a shallow pond left by a rain. The members of this wild Australian tribe are completely dependent on such chance sources of water as this pool. It was left by a sudden downpour and will quickly evaporate. The Bindibu have neither drinking cups nor pots

to store spare water in. Instead, they rely on their knowledge of where water probably will be found. Also, they
are used to getting along without water if they must.

In times of drought, they chew plants to obtain moisture.
They may spend days hiking many miles to find hidden
springs or puddles like this one to get water to drink.

A herd of sheep crosses Grand
Coulee Dam, which holds back the
Columbia River in eastern Wash-
ington State. Water stored by the
dam has irrigated a million acres of
farmland in the Pacific Northwest.

8

Man Invades
the Desert

We have come a long way in our study of deserts. By
now many of the ideas you once had probably have been
changed. For example, you must now be aware that deserts
are really not so deserted after all. In the years ahead, they
will become even less deserted.

Way back in Chapter 1 we learned that if all the major
deserts of the world were grouped into one place, they
would cover an area larger than the whole continent of
South America. Until fairly recent times, the world's deserts
were considered useless. Most people thought of them as
wastelands where nothing would grow, and only a few people chose to live there. Nothing worth while was to be found
there.

Few people feel that way any more. Within this century
the deserts of the world have been found to contain great
riches. For example, about half the world's supply of oil is
believed to lie beneath the deserts. The deserts also contain
great stores of minerals—nitrates, phosphates and borax,
along with copper, silver and uranium.

However, if water were brought to the desert by irrigation

and crops were made to grow, this would be the desert's greatest treasure.

For centuries, people have been irrigating desert land. Today, irrigation is almost a specialized science. But the strange thing is that modern methods have done little to improve on the irrigation system perfected by some people who lived more than 2,000 years ago. It is an amazing story.

An Ancient Irrigation System

A short distance east of the Mediterranean Sea, in what is now Israel, there is a small, rocky desert called the Negev. It is a barren country of dry, rolling hills. Until recent times, there were almost no people living there.

But deep inside the Negev are the ruins of several ancient cities. They were the home of an Arab people called the Nabateans (Nab-a-*tee*-ans). Altogether about 10,000 people lived in the Negev.

A short distance to the east, in the barren hills of Jordan, have been found the ruins of a city called Petra. This was the capital of the Nabateans, and its ruins include hundreds of houses, temples, tombs and monuments, many of them carved out of beautiful rosy-red sandstone.

For many years, historians could not understand why the Nabateans had built their cities in the middle of nowhere, since of course nothing could be made to grow in the desert. The only answer seemed to be that these people had gotten

HOW MAN CAN MAKE A DESERT

UNTOUCHED LANDS

Even in dry climates, land untouched by man has plants and trees growing on it. Their roots hold the soil and help to prevent erosion of the area.

FARMING STARTS

Farming begins with cutting down the trees. Now there are few roots to hold the soil, and the plowed land is exposed to erosion by wind and water.

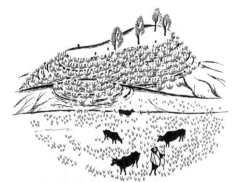

OVERFARMING

Too much farming and the loss of soil from erosion force the farms to move up onto the slopes. The flatlands are now good only for pasturing cattle.

their food from somewhere else. It must have been brought in by caravans.

But closer study showed that the Nabateans had actually been farmers. This brought up a new question: How could anybody grow enough food in the midst of the bleak Negev desert to feed 10,000 people?

There seemed to be only one answer. In the days of the Nabateans, the Negev must have been a fertile land. The climate must have turned dry after that time.

But during the 1930s, an American scientist explored these ruined cities and made a startling discovery: Nowhere in these buildings was there even a scrap of wood. No wood meant only one thing—there had never been any trees. In other words, the Negev in the days when Petra was a busy city was just as much of a desert as it is today.

The Nabatean Method

This led to more studies and even more startling discoveries about the way the Nabateans had managed to grow huge crops in the very center of the desert. All this, you must remember, was more than 2,000 years ago. Here is how they did it:

The area around Petra was a land of barren hills. And of course it was an area with very little rainfall—usually between two and four inches a year. As in many desert regions, the little rain that fell came once or twice a year in violent

OVERGRAZING

By now the slopes have been ruined by farming. Overgrazing has ruined the flatlands, leaving them bare of grass. Cows now graze on the slopes.

RUINED LAND

Continued cattle grazing, along with erosion from wind and water, finally leaves the area useful only for grazing goats—and they strip the hills clean.

NOW A DESERT

Finally all the topsoil is gone and big patches of bare rock are exposed. The land is so gullied by erosion that it is no longer able to support any life.

downpours. This rain, falling on the hard-baked ground, did not soak in. Instead it roared down the hillsides into dry gullies called wadies (*wah*-dees).

The rainwater from these violent storms poured through the wadies in flash floods which tore at the land. At most, these floods lasted only a few hours—then everything was dry once more.

Building Shelves for Farms

The marvelous thing the Nabateans did was to hit upon the idea of turning the wadies into farms. Basically, what they did was to slow down the floodwater as it came down the wadies during the brief, heavy rains. They managed this by building dozens and dozens of low rocky shelves down the dry wadi beds.

After that, when the rains came, they no longer roared uselessly downhill. Instead the water flowed down from one rocky shelf to the next, and the next—and so on.

The rainwater also washed down soil, and this was deposited on the shelves. As the years went by, more and more soil built up on these shelves, and they became a series of terraces, like a set of giant steps. In the hills, these terraces were small and narrow, but they widened out as they reached the valley below.

Where the wadies were too narrow for shelves, the Nabateans built many small dams. The purpose of these dams was to slow down the flow of water. The water then overflowed the banks of the wadies and spilled out over the land on either side. In this way, the land on both sides of the wadies was watered.

These "spillovers" and terraces were where the Nabateans did their farming. All together, these farms covered thousands of acres. Here the Nabateans grew vegetables, grain, dates, grapes and figs.

This ancient irrigation system amazes experts today. One reason is that the Nabateans used small terraces to catch water for their needs instead of building one large dam to store water. A single large dam would have been much more difficult for the Nabateans to build, and would have provided only enough water to irrigate a much smaller area of ground.

This ancient irrigation system worked so well that it is being copied today. In Israel, for example, where about half the country is in the Negev, there are farms irrigated by systems almost exactly the same as those the Nabateans used.

It is amazing that the Nabateans were able to build such an irrigation system. But they were more than good engineers. They solved one problem that some modern irrigation engineers have overlooked. This was the important matter of drainage. Without proper drainage, irrigation can actually ruin crops.

As recently as 1949, an irrigation system was built in Turkey without proper drainage. The result was that each time the fields were irrigated, the water brought in was allowed to stand until it evaporated in the air.

When the water evaporated, it left salts behind. In time the fields became so salty that crops would no longer grow. Irrigation had actually ruined the land.

Irrigation presents one other important problem, and this is when water from desert wells is used.

Under the ground there are two sources of water. One source is underground *rivers*. These buried rivers are fed constantly by rain and melting snow from distant mountains. When a well is drilled down into one of these rivers, it is not likely to go dry.

But underground *pools* are the usual source of well water. These pools take centuries to form. Here the water has been trapped in a layer of rock. Very little if any new water enters these pools. If water is constantly pumped out of them, sooner or later the pools will go dry.

A Possible Danger

For this reason, experts are afraid that the underground water will be used up. They do not yet know whether the use of these underground pools will prove to be unwise.

Recently there has been great interest in experiments to make salty sea water into fresh water. So far, most methods have proved too expensive for the process to be used on a large scale. But by some time in the 1970s, it is thought that

U.S. NATIONAL PARKS AND MONUMENTS IN DESERT AREAS

Name and Location	Acreage
Arches, Utah	34,249
Aztec Ruins, N. Mex.	27
Bandelier, N. Mex.	27,103
Big Bend, Tex.	708,221
Bryce Canyon, Utah	36,010
Canyon de Chelley, Ariz.	83,840
Capitol Reef, Utah	37,172
Carlsbad Caverns, N. Mex.	49,447
Casa Grande, Ariz.	472
Chaco Canyon, N. Mex.	21,509
Chiricahua, Ariz.	10,645
Death Valley, Calif.-Nev.	1,907,760
El Morro, N. Mex.	1,278
Gila Cliff Dwellings, N. Mex.	160
Gran Quivira, N. Mex.	610
Grand Canyon, Ariz.	673,575
Great Sand Dunes, Colo.	36,740
Hovenweep, Utah-Colo.	505
Joshua Tree, Calif.	557,934
Montezuma Castle, Ariz.	842
Natural Bridges, Utah	2,649
Navajo, Ariz.	360
Organ Pipe Cactus, Ariz.	330,874
Petrified Forest, Ariz.	94,161
Rainbow Bridge, Utah	160
Saguaro, Ariz.	63,284
Tonto, Ariz.	1,120
Tuzigoot, Ariz.	42
Walnut Canyon, Ariz.	1,879
White Sands, N. Mex.	146,535
Wupatki, Ariz.	35,693
Zion, Utah	147,034

100 billion gallons of salty sea water can be turned into fresh water every day—and so cheaply that this water can be used for irrigation.

So far we have looked at the desert only as a place to find minerals and as a place to be turned into farmland. But there is another way in which the desert can be used. That is as a great grazing land for herds of animals. Experts believe that about half of all the earth's arid areas could provide pastureland for at least some livestock. If all those areas were carefully looked after, they would help to add a great deal to the world's supply of food. Let us look at two cases of the use of dry lands for grazing animals.

Our first example shows careless use of land. In an area of East Africa, native herders moved in and began killing off the wild animals to get more pastureland for cattle and to get rid of a deadly disease called rinderpest, which is similar to the sleeping sickness that kills people. Rinderpest is carried by a parasite in the blood of wild animals. It does not hurt them, but the disease kills cattle. The deadly parasite is spread from animal to animal by the tsetse fly (*tset*-see). And so, to make the region safe for their cattle, the herders killed off the wild animals.

At first, the cattle did well. But, as so often happens, it was not long before the grassland was being overgrazed. Eventually the land became dry and useless.

Wise Use of Land

Our second example shows wise use of land. There were once huge herds of saiga antelope roaming the plains of southern Russia. Early in this century, the saiga were almost extinct. For years, people had hunted the saiga and herds of livestock had been turned loose on their grazing grounds. Then, in 1919, the government decided to save these rare antelope.

Hunting saiga was made illegal and the cattle were removed from the land. In a few years the number of antelope increased greatly, until there were hundreds of thousands of them. Today the herds are so large that saiga can be used, like cattle, for their meat and hides. Not only that, but the

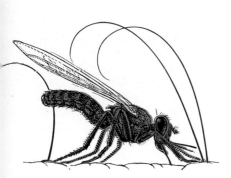

THE TSETSE FLY

This insect's name is pronounced "*tset*-see." It is shown here (magnified) in the act of biting. These little African flies are the carriers of sleeping sickness, which often kills humans. An infected person becomes dull and feels weary all the time. The last stage is a kind of deep sleep, followed by death.

plant life in the area is in far better shape now than when smaller herds of livestock grazed there.

The lesson to be learned here is a simple one. First of all, the use of dry grasslands for raising cattle can actually turn these lands into deserts. In some cases, it may be easier to leave the wild animals on the land and treat them as if they were farm animals. That means using their flesh for food and their hides for leather.

In other words, to get the most from the land it may be necessary to change *nothing* there. All that needs changing is our *thinking*. It may be far wiser to raise a herd of wild animals than a herd of cattle.

Looking to the Future

And so we have nearly come to the end of our story. Is your head full of desert facts about rainfall and seeds and kangaroo rats and erosion? Perhaps so. But it would be too bad to think of deserts only in terms of these things. They are all part of the story of deserts—but they are not the whole story. There is also the beauty of the deserts.

Unfortunately deserts have always had a bad name. Deserts are said to be "terrible" or "harsh" or "dangerous." Deserts are thought of as places where people get lost and die horribly of thirst. Deserts are the home of vultures and rattlesnakes and scorpions.

All this is unfair, because deserts are actually among the most beautiful places on earth. For every dust storm there are a hundred cloudless days when the air is so clean and clear it even smells different from the air in other places. There is almost no limit to the distance you can see. For every rattlesnake there are a hundred delightful and harmless little desert animals. And for every person who ever died of thirst in the desert, there are thousands who have lived their entire lives there as safely as people in any modern American city.

It is true that deserts are places of great emptiness. A person on foot could go for days without ever seeing a sign of another human being. But there is something quite thrilling about such emptiness. Only in a place so huge and so empty

THE SAIGA ANTELOPE

This stocky animal is found in the desert plains of southern Russia, where the summers are very hot and the winters bitter cold. The saiga was once in danger of dying out. It is now protected by law. Its large nose is so formed that it keeps the animal from breathing sand as it feeds on desert grasses.

does a person begin to realize how really small he is. There is a saying that you never know how little you are until you look at a mountain. The emptiness of deserts is much the same—and it is breathtaking.

In recent years, people have begun to realize this. They have grown tired of life in cities, with their smoky air and crowds of people. The deserts offer a place to live with fresh air to breathe and room to move about.

As a result, thousands of people have moved into homes in the desert. Wells have been drilled to obtain water, and electricity has brought in the means to air-condition homes.

In certain parts of the American Southwest, the sudden arrival of all these new settlers has upset some people. They see the day when deserts will have many factories and millions of residents.

The Fear of Desert Crowding

There are some good reasons for such fears. During World War II, between 1941 and 1945, the advantages of plenty of space and a year-round supply of fresh air were realized. Large factories were built in the deserts. Many of these factories made products for the aircraft industry. For them, a clean, dust-free atmosphere was important. With the factories, of course, came homes for the workers to live in. Today, still more factories are being built. Some desert lovers believe that in time the wild beauty of the deserts will be destroyed in this way.

What about the future, then? Nobody knows. But it seems fairly sure that more and more people will be moving into the desert. Whether they will treat it wisely or whether they will ruin it is hard to say.

Unfortunately mankind does not have a very good record. He has been known to spoil much more than he has improved. But there have been exceptions. There have been people like the Nabateans, who actually made the desert bloom. The same is true in parts of the American deserts. The Imperial Valley, one of this country's most highly productive areas, was made fertile through irrigation and wise use of the land.

THE BLADE OF A GIANT PLOW TOWERS ABOVE THREE MEN. IT IS USED TO LEVEL GROUND FOR IRRIGATION

Desert Wealth

More and more, modern man is finding how to make use of deserts. With new tools and the discoveries of science, he is able to find new sources of water, which permit rich crops to grow. The deserts are also rich in minerals, and they contain a wealth of natural beauty, as many people are now learning.

173

California's Man-made Oasis

Some of the world's richest farmland is in the Colorado Desert, in California's Imperial Valley. Sixty years ago the valley itself was as dry as the desert areas that still surround it. Now Colorado River water flows along a canal to the low-lying valley. There the water combines with the rich soil and unending sunshine to bring forth crops the year round—a great modern example of desert land put to use by irrigation.

THE ALL-AMERICAN CANAL flows in a concrete trench through the Colorado Desert. It carries millions of gallons of Colorado River water to irrigate the lush farms of the Imperial Valley. The canal was begun in 1934 and took six years to complete.

MUD-LADEN WATERS pass through six basins which remove mud and silt from Colorado River water on its way to irrigate the Imperial Valley.

RICH FIELDS of the Imperial → Valley (right) yield $150 million in crops from 650,000 desert acres made into fertile land by means of irrigation.

A MODERN MILL is needed to separate uranium from the rock ore in which it is found. This one is located on the barren Colorado Plateau. The process of refining uranium is very complicated. The ore must be crushed, screened, soaked in chemicals, roasted and dissolved out. The final product is a small amount of uranium in the form of

THIS SMILING NAVAJO INDIAN, Paddy Martinez, had luck as a prospector. He struck a huge uranium deposit in New Mexico. Mining firms pay him $250 a month for life.

Minerals in the Desert

The Colorado Plateau is a vast area in the American Southwest. For centuries, few people lived there. But in the 1950s, the area was suddenly invaded by thousands of outsiders looking for uranium, one of the chief sources of atomic energy. A huge quantity of this rare mineral ore had been found under the Colorado Plateau, and the Government was offering a high price for it.

But the dream of these uranium hunters lasted for only a year or two. They soon discovered that uranium is not like silver or gold, which are sometimes found in almost pure nuggets. Uranium is usually found in tiny quantities mixed up with huge amounts of rock. Therefore mining and separating uranium from the rock in which it is found require a quantity of expensive machinery.

"yellow cake." Other valuable minerals are found in the same ore. One is the metal vanadium, which goes into the making of jet engines. It is also used to harden steel tools.

NEXT PAGES: In Chile's Atacama Desert, the terraced → Anaconda copper mine produces 300,000 tons of copper yearly, more than any other copper mine in the world.

Valuable Salts in Desert Lakes

A glass of water taken from Utah's Great Salt Lake will leave an inch of white salt in the bottom of the glass when the water has evaporated. The lake and its nearby marshes are the remains of an inland sea and contain about six billion tons of salt. Getting this salt is a big business. Much of it is plain table salt; some, however, also contains potash. Searles Dry Lake in California (*right*) is rich in borax as well.

A PADDLE WHEEL moves salty water from a Bonneville Salt Flats marsh to an evaporating pool. The paddle wheel is needed because salt clogs even the best pumps.

A FINE SPRAY of salty water makes a mist over Searles ➤ Dry Lake in California. The salty water is pumped from underground and the water is evaporated on the surface.

A Rich Desert Gift

More than half of the oil in the world is found beneath deserts. This huge supply of oil is necessary to keep modern machinery running. The work of recovering this supply has led to the development of a new, specialized technology. In Algeria, wells have been sunk two miles deep. Pipelines a thousand miles long have been laid through Saudi Arabia *(right)*. Oil towns have sprung up in lonely places. Heat and drought add to the oilman's problems. Yet desert wells yield six million barrels daily.

DRUMS OF OIL stretch in long lines toward a storage depot at Ras Tanura, Saudi Arabia. The oil shown here is for local use only. It is a small part of the total output.

BURNING GAS FLARES LIGHT THE DESERT NIGHT AT THIS SAHARAN OIL FIELD. GAS IS FOUND UNDERGROUND

A DESERT PIPELINE a thousand miles long, being built above, can pipe 479,000 barrels of oil daily across Saudi Arabia. The oil line saves a nine-day trip by sea through the Suez Canal and into the Mediterranean Sea. Pipe was brought to the site in 93-foot lengths that were then welded together on the spot. The line was opened in 1950.

WITH THE OIL. IN SOME OIL FIELDS, NATURAL GAS IS USED FOR POWER, AND THE SURPLUS IS BURNED OFF

SIGNPOSTS AT A DESERT CROSSROAD point the way to homes newly built in the Mojave Desert in California. In the past few years, more than 250,000 new residents have moved into the Mojave. These new desert dwellers enjoy the bright desert sun and clear air. At one time desert land was cheap, but it is getting more expensive.

A REFRESHING POOL shines under the desert sun in a resort town in California. Many such resorts are being built. In the winter, the population just about doubles.

CAREFREE CHILDREN play happily on the dunes of → California's Death Valley *(right)*. Once it was a dreaded desert where travelers died. Now it is a tourist attraction.

Glossary

Acre. A measurement of land area (43,560 square feet, or slightly larger than a football field).

Adaptation. Adjustment of living things to their surroundings which improves their chances to survive.

Altitude. The height of an object or place above a certain level, which is usually sea level.

Arid. Without moisture, dry or barren. In an arid place the rainfall is barely enough for plants to grow.

Artesian well. A well that is like a natural fountain. Natural underground water pressure causes the water to flow up through a hole bored into the ground.

Atmosphere. The mass of air that surrounds the earth. It is many miles high.

Borax. A kind of salt found in deserts. It has many uses, including the making of glass.

Burrow. A hole in the ground dug by some animals for shelter.

Butte. A small isolated hill with steep sides and a flat top, left by the erosion of the land around it.

Canyon. A deep valley with high, steep slopes, formed by a river cutting through a dry region.

Caravan. In deserts, usually a band of travelers or traders on a journey.

Climate. The average weather conditions of an area over a period of time.

Condense. To change a substance from vapor to liquid.

Desert. Any area with generally high temperatures which gets little rainfall (less than 10 inches a year).

Dormant. A condition in which life is almost at a standstill, as in seeds.

Drought. A long period of very dry weather due to a lack of rain.

Dune. A hill or ridge of sand piled up by the wind.

Erosion. Gradual wearing away of land by water, ice or wind.

Evaporate. To change a substance from liquid to vapor.

Extinct. No longer living—having died out.

Fertile land. Land that produces abundant plants.

Geologist. A scientist who studies the earth, its layers of soil and rock, and their history.

Grub. The wormlike form of a beetle which hatches from the egg and later turns into an adult insect.

Gully. A narrow, deep channel in the ground with steep sides, formed by the runoff of heavy rains.

Gypsum. A common mineral which is used mainly for making plaster.

Hibernation. The very deep sleep of some animals in winter.

Instinct. An inherited pattern of behavior.

Irrigation. Artificial watering of land in order to grow crops.

Land form. Feature of the landscape, such as a hill, valley, mountain or rock formation.

Lava. Hot, fluid rock from inside the earth that flows to the surface, often through volcanoes. On the surface, it hardens.

Mammal. Any animal (including man) which has a backbone and is warm-blooded. Its young are born alive (not as eggs) and drink milk.

Mesa. A large, flat-topped hill left by erosion of the land around it.

Migration. Movement of animals from one place to another, frequently in large numbers.

Mirage. A kind of desert trick which makes travelers imagine they see such things as lakes in the distance (*pages 34 and 110-111*).

Nitrate. A chemical salt with many uses, including the making of explosives.

Nomad. A member of a tribe that wanders from place to place and has no permanent home.

Oasis. An area in the desert where water is found and plants grow.

Plain. A land area with a nearly flat or gently rolling surface.

Plateau. A high, flat land area with at least one side having steep slopes.

Playa. A salt flat. The Spanish word for beach.

Potash. A white chemical substance sometimes found in deserts. It is very valuable as a fertilizer.

Precipitation. Water which falls to earth from clouds as rain, snow, hail or sleet—but not as fog.

Rainfall (inches of rain). The term "inches of rain" is used to describe the amount of water which falls to earth. For example, one inch of rain would cover the ground to a depth of one inch—if it did not sink in or run off. The term "annual rainfall" refers to the number of inches of rain in the course of a year at a certain place.

Rain shadow. An inland area that gets little rain because it lies beyond a range of mountains which force moist air to rise and dry out.

Reptile. An animal such as a snake, lizard or crocodile that has a dry scaly body and lays eggs. Its body temperature depends on the temperature of its surroundings.

Rodent. A mammal such as a squirrel, rat or mouse that has teeth for gnawing and chewing. Rodents are the most numerous and widespread of mammals.

Salt flat. An area where water has dried up, leaving the ground covered with salts. Heavy rains turn it into a shallow, muddy lake.

Salt lake. In a dry region, a lake

186

with no outlet such as a stream or river. Rain water that washes down into the lake carries salt with it. The water then evaporates, leaving the salt behind, which makes the lake more and more salty.

Sediment. Sand, gravel, silt and other material eroded from rocks and deposited in seas, lakes and streams.

Succulent. A type of plant, such as a cactus, that stores water within its stem or leaves.

Terrain. A word meaning "land," but usually used to describe the general appearance of land, such as "mountain terrain" or "flat terrain."

Topsoil. The fertile layer of soil on the surface of the ground where plants grow. It is rarely more than three feet thick.

Wadi. The Arabic word for "wash."
Wash. Dry stream bed.
Weathering. The wearing away of the earth's surface by exposure to wind and water.

Picture Credits

Acknowledgments

The editors of this book are indebted to Charles H. Lowe Jr., Professor of Zoology, University of Arizona; James Matthai, Associate Professor of Geography, Murray State College, Murray, Kentucky; George F. Adams, Professor of Geology, City College of New York; Laurence K. Marshall and the Peabody Museum, Harvard University; Arthur N. Strahler, Professor of Geomorphology, Columbia University; Donald F. Thomson, Professor of Anthropology, Melbourne University; Colin M. Turnbull, Assistant Curator of African Ethnology, The American Museum of Natural History, New York City; Lewis Wayne Walker, Associate Director, Arizona-Sonora Desert Museum, Tucson; and Maitland Edey, Editor, the LIFE Nature Library and its staff.

Index

Numerals in italic type indicate pages that include a photograph or painting of the subject mentioned.

Index